Simplified Taoism and Buddhism: Essential Guide to Inner Peace

Misty .C Deacon

Funny helpful tips:

Establish boundaries; they protect the sanctity of the relationship.

Engage with books that promote a growth mindset; they foster a belief in personal evolution and potential.

Simplified Taoism and Buddhism: Essential Guide to Inner Peace : Discover the Transformative Power of Taoism and Buddhism for Deep Inner Peace and Freedom

Life advices:

Maintain a strong online presence; digital visibility is crucial in today's market.

Engage with books that challenge societal norms; they stimulate critical thinking and societal progress.

Introduction

This book offers an introductory exploration of two ancient philosophies and their core concepts.

The book begins by defining Buddhism and tracing its origins in Hindu India. It addresses the question of whether there are gods in Buddhism and explains the role of gods within the belief system. Concepts like heaven, hell, and the three jewels of Buddhism are explored, providing insight into the beliefs that form the foundation of Buddhism.

The role of art in Buddhism is highlighted, shedding light on the significance of artistic expression within the tradition. The book also touches upon the relationship between Buddhism and cognitive science, emphasizing how Buddhist teachings contribute to the understanding of consciousness.

Readers are introduced to the historical figures who played pivotal roles in spreading Buddhism in China and Japan, further contextualizing the development of Buddhism in East Asia. Essential aspects of Buddhism, including symbols and their significance, are discussed, with a focus on the lotus symbol.

The book briefly explores the appeal of Buddhism to individuals from various backgrounds, including Christians, and distinguishes between different branches and sects of Buddhism. It addresses the question of whether Buddhism is a religion or a philosophy, offering insights into its unique perspective on happiness and life.

Common questions about Buddhism are answered, covering topics such as its origin, the process of becoming a Buddhist, key concepts, and the importance of meditation. The book also provides reasons why one should learn about Buddhism, highlighting its appeal and uniqueness.

Transitioning to Taoism, the book delves into Chinese Taoist wisdom for the modern day. It introduces the basic principles of Taoism, including Tao, De or Te, Wu Wei, and P U, offering readers a foundational understanding of Taoist philosophy.

Taoist meditation is explored, emphasizing the importance of meditation in Taoist practice. The book touches on Taoist spirituality and its potential application in psychotherapy, demonstrating how Taoist principles can be relevant to modern life.

The historical roots of Taoism are discussed, along with its connections to Chinese philosophy, medicine, and stress relief techniques. The book explores the differences between the modern Taoist regime and Western management theory, emphasizing concepts like "Salt Up" and Wei Wu Wei.

In summary, this book provides a comprehensive overview of Buddhism and Taoism, making these philosophies accessible to readers seeking an introductory understanding. It explores their core principles, historical backgrounds, and relevance in today's world, making it a valuable resource for beginners interested in these ancient traditions.

Contents

What is Buddhism?

What is Buddhism? Many consider Buddhism as a religion, although some deny the name because Buddhism does not teach the worship of gods. They say that Buddhism is a philosophy or just a way of life. This difference between religion and philosophy has emerged among Western commentators because the difference between the two is unclear in Asia, where it originated. It is true that, according to some sources, there are about 500 million followers in the world, making it the third-largest religion (if you can call it that).

The name Buddhism comes from the name of Siddhartha Gautam by his followers. They Called him the Buddha, which means "awakened" or "enlightened."Siddhartha Gautama lived in Northern India for about 500 B.C. He was a Prince of the Shakya tribe. He is widely known in the Buddhist world as Shakyamuni, the wise Shakya. These are the only historical facts we have about the Buddha. To know his teachings and his life, we must now look at him through the Buddhist eyes.

According to tradition, he lived as a Prince in the palace until the age of 29. His father took too much care of him. Throughout his life in the palace, he had not seen pain or suffering. However, at this point in his life, he saw for the first time the suffering of the human condition. He saw a sick man, an old man, and a dead body. He asked his servant, and he said that we were all going to suffer.

I say all this because we need to understand what questions Buddhism is trying to answer. The Buddha discovered the source and solution to the problem of human suffering. He said that everything in life causes suffering in one way or another. Then he said that this suffering happens because we are attached to things. This attachment comes from our ignorance and delusion.

Then I started talking about solving this problem. He said that Nirvana is the solution to the problem. Nirvana means to breathe out. The very disappearance of all our desires leads to the fact that our life continues a painful cycle. It is difficult to think of Nirvana as a positive goal from the point of view of the Western world, but for Buddhists, it is very desirable.

So is the Buddha trying to end human suffering? He didn't answer questions about the highest origin of reality or about our relationship with the gods, he just tried to solve the real problem that he found in life.

Considering Buddhism from this point of view, it is difficult to speak of it as a religion. This is more like a philosophy, or even shares some aspects with modern psychology.

However, if we look at how Buddhism is practiced around the world, we will not doubt how religious people perform their rituals. Mahayana Buddhists have completely changed the beliefs and practices of what can be considered traditional Buddhism. Some varieties of Mahayana worship the Bodhisattva and the celestial Buddha. These are beings who have attained enlightenment or the advanced path of the practitioner. They have the ability to intervene in this world to save people as if they were gods.

Thus, Buddhism is a very complex tradition. It can be viewed as a religion or something else, depending on how they view it.

The most basic Buddhist expression of faith is called Triple refuge: "I accept refuge in Buddy, I accept refuge in Dharma (doctrine), and I accept refuge in Sangi (community of Buddhist disciples).

To begin studying Buddhism, we must consider each of these three refuges. Let's start with the Buddha himself. The Buddha is often depicted sitting in a very quiet position, crossing his legs in front of him, and bending his hands on his knees. This is the very image of calm and contemplation. That is, this is an image that attracts many people and in the Buddha. The Buddha is an image of calm and tranquility in a confused and distracted world.

Another refuge is Dharma or learning. This teaching is presented in a doctrinal formula known as the Four Noble Truths: the truth of suffering, the origin of suffering, the cessation of suffering, and to the end.

Buddha did not stand still all his life. He needs to get up and create a student community. Places where the main events of the Buddha's life is still a pilgrimage center.

In India, there were two major reformist movements that appeared in the ancient history of Buddhism and changed the face of tradition. The first was called Mahayaya, "the Ferris wheel."It included a massive reorganization of basic Buddhist values. The second part was called Tantra. It has complicated this tradition; you can visit the link to my site at the end of the article to find out.

As Buddhism has spread to other Asian countries, it has continued to develop amazingly. It was brought by Buddhist missionaries to Sri Lanka. From there, it was brought to much of Southeast Asia. Buddhism entered China and developed distinctive traditions that interact with pre-existing local traditions. China, as you may know, is an extremely robust and courageous civilization, and Buddhism was not easily accepted because it was a foreign formation. However, there was a kind of kinship between Buddhist teachings and some aspects of Chinese culture.

From China, Buddhism was transferred to Korea, Japan, and then Vietnam. In the XIX century, Buddhism was transferred across the Himalayas from India to Tibet. Today, the Dalai Lama, leader of the Tibetan Buddhist community, is one of the most active leaders in the world. In many respects, it is a living symbol of Buddhism itself.

Today Buddhism has spread to the rest of the world, including Europe, Australia, and America. In some places, Buddhism is stronger in ethnic communities, such as Sri Lanka Buddhist Sangha in Los Angeles.

The Origin of Buddhism in Hindu India

The brahmins claim to lead the religious life and thought of India and outside of Islam may be said to have achieved their ambition, but at the cost of tolerating much, that the majority would like to suppress. But in the early centuries, their influence was less extensive, and there were other currents of religious activity, some hostile and some simply independent. The most formidable of these found expression in Jainism and Buddhism that arose in the sixth century B.C., this century was a time of intellectual ferment in many countries. In China, it produced Lao-Tseu and Confucius: In Greece, Parmenides, Empedocles, and sophists were only a little later. In all these regions, we have the same phenomenon as restless, wandering teachers, ready to give advice on politics, religion, or philosophy, to anyone who listens to them.

In Gautama's youth, Bihar was full of wandering philosophers who seem to have been atheists and willing to support the boldest, intellectual, and moral paradoxes. There must, however, be constructive elements in their doctrine, because they believed in the reincarnation and periodic appearance of superhuman teachers and in the advantage of following an ascetic discipline. They mainly belonged to the warrior caste as Gautama, the Buddha is known from history.

The Pitakas represent him as different in detail from contemporary teachers, but as rediscovering the truth taught by his predecessors. They imply that the world is so composed that there is only one way of emancipation and that from time to time, the higher spirits see it and announce it to others. Yet Buddhism does not use in practice formulas such as living in harmony with the laws of nature.

Indian literature is notoriously interested in ideas rather than facts, but the vigorous personality of the Buddha impressed upon her a more distinct portrait than that left by any other teacher or King. His work had a double effect. First, it influenced all departments of Hindu religion and thought, even those who nominally oppose it. Secondly, it spread not only Buddhism in the strict sense, but Indian art and literature beyond the limits of India. The expansion of Hindu culture owes much to the doctrine that the good law should be preached to all nations.

Are There gods in Buddhism?

Do Buddhists believe in God or gods? Buddhism is still considered unique and special among religions because its practitioners do not believe in a creator god, or at least, not rely on him for their salvation. According to the Pali Canon, the oldest Buddhist scriptures, The Buddha did not refuse the existence of the gods, but considered them subject to change and death. He said that invoking their help or influence was useless.

The truths of Buddhism do not depend on the gods, and attempts to use their influence, are depreciated as vulgar practices. So, faith in the gods is not essential in Buddhism, they can not help you achieve Nirvana. In fact, early Buddhists considered the human condition more favorable for the search for enlightenment, because the life of a god is full of distractions, and it is more difficult to focus on meditation and wisdom.

However, there is another side to the story. As Buddhism developed and evolved, its beliefs and practices changed radically. Mahayana Buddhists believe in heavenly bodhisattvas and Buddhas. They are beings who reside in the heavens and have infinitely greater power than us. These celestial bodhisattvas have the ability to intervene in this world and save people as if they were gods. These powers allow the celestial boddhisattvas to reside in the heavens, hence the Heavenly name. These powers also allow them to function as Buddhist equivalents of the Hindu gods.

Buddhists insist, however, that these great boddhisattvas have gone so far from the Hindu gods in their power and understanding of reality, that it is not appropriate to regard them as gods at all.

The Role of Gods in Buddhism

The attitude of the first Buddhism to the spirit world is special. Their existence was assumed, but the truths of religion do not depend on them and try to use their influence on victims, and oracles are condemned as vulgar practices like juggling. Later, Buddhism was infected with mythology, and critical changes occurred when deities, rather than just protecting the church, actively participated in the cause of salvation. When the Hindu gods developed into a person who could appeal to religious and philosophical thought as a cosmic force as the bearer of truth and lead to bliss, this example was too attractive to be ignored, and a Pantheon of Bodhisattvas was formed. But it is clear that when the Buddha preached in Kosala and Magadhi, the local deities did not reach this position. The philosophical systems of the time were mostly theistic, and oddly enough, religion had nothing to do with the gods.

Often, like the character of Dave in early Buddhist stories, the meaning of their appearance is almost always in their relationship with Budha or His disciples. There are several simple mythologies, such as Brahma and Indra, associated with other gods. In fact, the gods, although freely referred to as AIDS, are not taken seriously, and there are extremely curious passages in which the Buddha seems to laugh at them, just as the eighteenth-century skeptics laughed at the Yehas.

So, the kevaddhasutte tells how a monk, confused by a metaphysical problem, turned to various gods and eventually approached Brahma in the presence of all his followers. Hearing the question, where did the element stop and leave no trace? Brahma replied: "I am the Great Brahma, the supreme, powerful, all-knowing, ruler, lord, ruler, creator, chief of all, of the appointment of each of his places, old times, the father of all who are and should be.""But," said the monk, "I didn't ask you, man, you are really all that you are saying now, but I am asking you where the four elements stop and leave no trace."Then the Great Brahma took him by the hand, drew him aside, and said: "these gods think that I know and understand everything. So, I didn't answer in their presence. But I don't know the answer to your question, and you need to ask the Buddha."

Heaven and Hell in Buddhism

Buddhism speaks of many sub-worlds, of which Avicci is the most terrible. These are, of course, only temporary, and then Purgatory, rather than places of eternal punishment, and the beings that inhabit them, have the strength to fight and get credit, but this is a difficult task, and can be born repeatedly in hell. The phraseology of Buddhism refers to existence in heaven and hell as a new birth. It is more natural to say that some people are reborn as people, and others go to heaven or hell. But their destinies are really parallel.

The desire to welcome influential ideas, although they may be incompatible with the strict teaching of the Buddha, is well seen in the position that is given to the spirits of the dead. The Buddha was tireless in his condemnation of all the thoughts that suggest that a kind of soul or double escape from the body after death and continues to exist. But the belief in the existence of deceased ancestors and the presentation of victims to them was still part of the Hindu domestic religion.

To satisfy this persistent faith, Buddhism recognized the world of whores; they are ghosts. Many of them are described in the following books. Some are thin like faded leaves and suffer from constant hunger because their mouth is so small that they can not take solid food. According to strict theology are pet as category of beings just above animals, and some forms of bad behavior include the birth between them. But, according to the general estimate, only the spirits of the dead can receive food and other benefits.

Beliefs in Buddhism

Buddhists do not believe in a particular God. They do not believe that God interferes with everyday life; he lives by certain laws and rules. Five ethical rules - "fundamental laws":

- You won't kill any living thing.

- Don't steal.

- Don't abuse me.

- You're not going tolie.

- Do not drink alcohol or other substances that harm the body and soul.

The three jewels of Buddhism recite:

- I'll take my shelter in Buddy.

- I tend towards Dharma (teachings of Buddhism)

- I took refuge in the Sangha (monastic community)

If life is a disease, Buddhists believe that the Buddha is a "medicine"

There are many movements in Buddhism. Basic guidelines:

Theravada Buddhism. As the oldest teachings of Buddhism. Tripitaka istheir sacred texts. Monks teach the teachings of the Buddha. They also determine whether the texts are real, and that is the true text of the Buddha. They must approve the texts. The Buddhists of Theravada learn that Siddhartha was inspired by another Buddha to achieve enlightenment before the Prince's birth. And there is no one who can contact him, which means there is no reason to worship him. Historical Buddha, this one here is called "Gautama Buddha."This destination is widespread in Burma, Thailand, Laos, Cambodia, and Sri Lanka.

Mahayana Buddhism. Tripitak's letters are here too. But they also have a lotus tomorrow, which is a more recent text on the Buddha. Where the Buddha illuminates the entire universe. Mahayana Buddhists call the type of historical Buddha Shakyamuni. They believe that the historical Buddha has achieved enlightenment for millions of years. They believe that it is very important for people to work on themselves to achieve awakening. They emphasize generosity, tolerance, care, kindness, and courage. The nuns here have a great status. This destination is widespread in Mongolia, Tibet, Vietnam, and South Korea.

Zen Buddhism. The most important thing for Zen Buddhists is meditation. Otherwise, Zen Buddhists are similar to other directions. This trend was widely used in China, but at that time, it was common in Japan and Korea.

Lamaism. This direction is colorful and has many gods and goddesses. They dance in costume to scare away evil spirits. They also have prayer wheels where people can come and pray as they spin the prayer wheels. This direction is widespread in Mongolia, China, and Japan.

Art in Buddhism

Buddhist art flourished during the 2nd century B.C. when sculpture became clearer and represented the whole life of the Buddha Gautum and his teachings in the form of episodes of sculptures. It took the form of friezes as part of the decoration of Stupa. In India from where Buddhism actually began, Buddha was never shown in human form, but through its symbols. The reluctance to show Buddha in human form was due to many of his words that are mentioned in "Dighanikaya," which discouraged showing himself in human form after his disappearance.

The human representation of the Buddha began in the first century A.D.in northern India. The two main creative centers have been identified in the "Gandhara" in the north-western border province of Pakistan and in the "Mathura" region in North-Central India. The Art of Gandhara emerged due to the centuries of influence of the Greeks since the conquest of Alexander The Great in 332 B.C. The influence of Greek sculpture is widely visible in Gandharan Buddhist sculpture. The contribution of Gandharan sculpture has added wavy hair, shoulder-covering draperies, sandals and shoes, Acanthus leaf decorations, etc. where such strong Indian traditions can be widely seen in Mathura art that is illustrated by the representation of Buddha in human form with deities like yaksas. Mathura art also added clothes covering the left shoulder, wheel on Palm, Lotus seat, etc.

Buddhist art continued to develop in India for a few centuries, and Mathura's pink sandstone sculpture evolved during the Gupta period (from the 4th to the 6th century) and reached very high fineness and delicacy. In the 10th century, his creations died in India due to the rapid progression of Hinduism and Islam, but Buddhist art flourished outside the Indian subcontinent when it expanded in the 1st century A.D. His artistic nature merges with other sculptures of countries that have adopted faith. Buddhist art prevailed in the form of Buddhism" Mahayana " towards the North Road to Central Asia, Tibet, Bhutan, China, Korea, Japan, and Vietnam. While Buddhism "Theravada" prevailed on the southern road to Myanmar, Thailand, and Cambodia.

In the first century A.D., the transmission of Buddhist art was made in Central Asia, China, and finally Korea and Japan when an embassy was sent to the West by the Chinese Emperor Ming (58-75 ad). However, the correct transmission began in the II century A.D.with the expansion of the Kushan Empire on the Chinese territory of the Tarim Basin and with the efforts of a large number of Central Asian Buddhist monks in the Chinese lands. The fusion of different cultures in art on its way of expansion has added new impacts on Buddhist art. This can be seen in the area where it has expanded. As in China, the Buddhist regime has a strong impact on

Chinese traits and culture. Their historical prints can be seen in the Buddhist art of China. Similarly, their Stupa hasstrong Chinese impacts of Tang Buddhist art.

Korean Buddhist art reflects the interaction of Chinese Buddhist influence and pure original Korean culture. Steppe art is evident in Korean Buddhist art based on the excavation of artifacts and funeral goods such as Silla Royal Crowns, belt buckles, daggers, and comma-shaped gogok. In Tibet, Tantric Buddhism began as a movement of India in the 5th or 6th century. It was derived from Brahmanism. Tibetan Buddhist art received the influence of Indian, Nepalese, and Chinese Art. One of the most characteristic creations of Tibetan Buddhist art is the mandalas, diagrams of a "divine temple" made of a circle that surrounds a square. Vietnam also has a strong Chinese Buddhist influence. Similarly, Myanmar, Thailand, and Cambodia have a direct Indian influence on their Buddhist art.

Japan being geographically at the end of the Silk Road, had many influences before the advent of Buddhism. Japan, the largest Buddhist country today, discovered Buddhism in the 6th century when Buddhist missionary monks came to the islands with various works of art and sculptures. The country adopted Buddhism in the following century. Japan was able to preserve many aspects of Buddhism just as it disappeared in India, and be suppressed in Central Asia and China only because of its geographical location.

Quite simply, if we carefully examine the footprints of history, we can clearly see that Buddhist art known today in many parts of the world has actually evolved from its original form. Every country or society that practices Buddhism today has introduced new things according to their way of life. The cultural impact of different societies on Buddhist art is evident from the careful study of history and society. From the shape and order of the Stupa to the appearance of the Buddha, everything was personalized by the sculpture of time. Originally stupas were painted and decorated in such a way that the whole life of the Sidharta Gautama (Buddha) was shown step wise so that disciples could seek advice. Later, each society influenced Buddhist art with its own cultural heritage. Each society left its mark on Buddhist art and evolved it the way it wanted.

Reality of Buddhism

As a pure Catholic, I believe in the true law of our Creator. But then there is always an exception to the rule.

Buddhism is a gentle and peaceful religion that has survived 25 centuries of non-violence. Religion is based on the teachings of Siddharth Gautama, the son of a powerful ruler who lived a very luxurious life in his father's palace in northern India. At the age of 29, this man saw for the first time the sufferings and pains of his life. Because of this, he began to think deeply about the nature of illness and death from old age. In search of the cause of this suffering, Siddharth left his life in luxury and embraced the life of a wandering ascetic. After a while, he realized that the research was not based on the safety of his old way of life.

Not finding an answer or extreme, Siddhartha began a new search, "the middle way." The middle way is a dynamic teaching, as evidenced by the traditional history of the Buddha. This is the path between the extremes of indulgence and self-confidence. He began to eat so that hunger no longer occupied his thoughts and sat under the Bodhi tree to meditate. Under Bodhi, Siddhartha found what he was looking for, enlightenment. Siddhartha was born as Buddha or is known as "enlightened."He went to the city of Benares, where he began to talk about his enlightenment and four noble truths, namely:

Suffering is: the whole life is full of suffering.

There is a reason to suffer. Suffering comes from the desire for everyday things.

There is a way to end suffering. Suffering stops when a person overcomes a selfish desire.

One way to end suffering by an enlightened path - you can learn how to end desire by following 8 Rules:

Good opinions are to know and understand the Four Noble Truths.

Good thoughts to let go of his needs and desires.

Good speech tells the Truth, Speak softly and wisely.

It's good to act politely so as not to hurt anything.

The right to an existential minimum is to earn a living that does not harm others.

The effort is simply to encourage and nurture positive thinking to keep pace.

Good awareness is to wake up with thoughts and actions that affect the world.

A good concentration is a calm thought that is born with good practice eight times.

For forty-five years, Buddha taught the people of North India, a means of enlightenment. He died in the 1980s. In the Life Of The Buddha, he showed no desire to support his learning.

From my point of view, I agree with this type of Chinese religious practice. To my knowledge, the virtues set forth in this practice do not violate any law of human morality. With them, people will continue to live their lives in peace without harming or violating the virtues of others. Life will be simple and live without a sense of fear.

Buddhism Teaches Cognitive Science About Consciousness

Suppose you see a red apple, and that is all your eye does for you. It simply brings you a sensual image of an Apple, somehow translates the outside world into an image for consciousness, but it does not give the idea that the image is an Apple, nor does it make the word "Apple" appear in mind. Who will come next? It somehow gives you a mental image of a red apple that reflects the outside world and transmits this reflection in mind. This is what reflects the appearance of consciousness: it gives you the shape, color, smell, feeling of an Apple, reflecting the outside world, and turning it into an image of consciousness.

So, what you see when you see an Apple is not an Apple, but a conscience. You see, perceive, witness, or experience only one image in your mind, but not the Apple itself. The image in mind does not give you any intelligence other than the image, so your eyes, ears, tongue, body, and nose give you all those mental impressions that Buddhism calls images or signs. Your five senses are like five soldiers who always report accurately to headquarters without adding comments or interpretations. They just give you all those simultaneous images. But who plays them?

Without being able to capture these images and distinguish them into parts with borders, properties, or features, you have no idea that there is anything out there with a specific value, such as a specific object with certain attributes and features. In other words, in addition to rejecting the external world than inside, consciousness has the function of discrimination, which makes this set of images very different from the point of view of the other set. Otherwise, everything looks identical.

Let us get our delicious apple back. The camera captures the image of the apple through the lens to the mirror, just like the image that passes through our cornea on our retina, but without the mind to comment on the camera lens or the mirror keeps the image in there. This image of the Apple camera is something completely incomprehensible to the camera and is the same as any other image because there is no intelligence to distinguish differences. In this way, you can see what consciousness reflects and distinguishes its consciousness. One aspect of consciousness gives us Images, and another gives us meaning.

The mirror instantly and indiscriminately reflects forms and images, and in the same way, our senses give consciousness such a set of reflections or nameless impressions. If you do not have a discriminatory mind, the images on the left resemble the images on the right. You could not tell them apart. Only discrimination can make them different from each other. This means that there is a part of consciousness that works to get individual objects out of chaos to make sense of what we call a discrimination function. The objective world is known or recognized for us by a part of consciousness that clearly defines individual forms, phenomena, or phenomena, and by these words, I mean sounds, physical sensations, smells, and so on.

So, you have a consciousness that distinguishes us from this palace's sensual experiences that cannot be decoded and are surrounded by words, names, and memory labels to do something recognizable. Discrimination as a function of consciousness includes phenomena that go beyond inseparable sensory consciousness, and the objective world discriminates in this phenomenon. This gives you an objective field of individual objects with independent characteristics. It brings personal judgments or reflections on this world, and it is done seemingly forever.

This is the first part of what Buddha Sakyamuni learned about consciousness. You have a current state of consciousness, and it has two aspects. The present consciousness consists of a reflexive and different consciousness. Consciousness also has a finite basis, and, through meditation, consciousness can be traced back to this finite root. It is that Buddhist meditation is its main goal.

Buddhism and the Government

Here I want to talk about the relationship between church and state. This is the simplest in Buddhism, which teaches that the truth is one, that all men should follow it, and that all good kings should respect and encourage it. This is also a Christian position, but Buddhism has almost always been tolerant and has almost not supported the doctrine that mistakes should be suppressed by force. Buddhism does not claim to cover the entire field of religion, as it is understood in Europe: if people like to calm spirits in the hope of obtaining wealth and crops, it allows them to do so.

In Japan and Tibet, Buddhism played a more secular role than in other countries, similar to the struggle of the medieval European Church for power. In Japan, the great monasteries became almost the main military leader and the main political power, and this danger was only avoided by the destruction of Hiizan and other major settlements in the 16th century.

What was prevented in Japan actually happened in Tibet, as the monasteries became stronger than all the competing secular factions, and the main sects established an ecclesiastical government individually, like the papacy. In southern countries such as Burma and Ceylon, Buddhism did not attempt to interfere in politics.

Buddhism and Hinduism have the idea that a monk or priest is a person who, because of ordination or birth, lives on a higher level than others. He can teach and do good, but it is nevertheless the duty of the laity to maintain the priesthood. This teaching preaches Hinduism in a stronger form than Buddhism. The intellectual superiority of the brahmin as caste was real enough to ensure its acceptance, and in politics, they had the good sense to run the service, to be Ministers, not kings. In theory, and to a great extent in practice, the brahmanis and their gods are not the Empire of an Empire, but the Empire of a super Empire. The situation was possible only because, unlike the Tibetan papacy and Lama, they had no Pope and no hierarchy. They produced neither beckets nor Hildebrands nor Inquisition. They did not quarrel with science but monopolized it.

The widely held view of church-state relations in China and Japan is almost the opposite of this. In these countries, there is only a hidden theory of the official world that religion is a public service, and that there should be rules for gods and worship, as well as for Ministers and labels. If we say that religion is identified with the government in Tibet and forms an Imperium in India, we can compare our position in the far East with the home States under British rule.

There is no interference with beliefs in accordance with the conventions for ethical and socially: I appreciate the teachings and ceremonies interesting: the government accepts and rewards the sincere cooperation of the priests, Buddhists, and Taoists, but reserves the right to limit his activity if he wants to have a bad policy or if an excessive increase in the Imperial government of China has succeeded in the claim, as it was reinforced and reduced not only by priests, but

In China and Japan, there was often a strong mood in the official classes against Buddhism, but on the other hand, it often had the support of emperors and peoples, and princes often joined the priesthood, especially when it was desirable to live in retirement. Confucianism and Shintoism, which are ethical and ceremonial rather than doctrinal, have, in the past, been to some extent the law for the governments of China and Japan, or more precisely, an aspect of these governments. But for centuries, far Eastern statesmen have rarely considered Buddhism and Taoism more than interesting and legitimate activities that should be encouraged and regulated as educational and scientific institutions.

Historical Figures Who Stabilized Buddhism in China and Japan

There are people we study in history classes in the upper classes. It is clear in what years they lived and what they did. These facts can be considered the X-axis of history. They form a horizontal chronological line using time as variables. But usually, we do not pay attention to people who lived at the same time, but in different places. These people can play an interactive role in the story. They form a vertical axis. Su can find interesting facts about history if we pay attention to the X and Y axes of history.

Today I thought about Buddhism. I know famous historical figures. I chose four key people in the history of Buddhism without paying attention to their age and discovered an interesting fact. Buddhism, a religion of Indian origin, spread in China between the first and second centuries. It became popular in China and was introduced to Korea in the fourth century and Japan in the sixth century. Here are four key features that stabilized Buddhism in China and Japan.

Xuanjiang was a Chinese monk. He went to India to obtain and deliver authentic Buddhist documents in China. (602-664 A.D.)

He Prince Shotoku, the Crown Prince of the Japanese Empire. He was the key man who brought Buddhism to Japan. He laid the foundation for the stabilization of Buddhism in Japan. (574-622 A.D.)

Jian Zhen (Ganjin in Japanese) was a Chinese monk. He spread and strengthened Buddhism in Japan. (688-763 A.D.)

Reflecting on the early days of Buddhism in China and Japan, I chose these people without knowing their chronology. This list shows that the spread of Buddhism from India to China and Japan occurred in a relatively short period between the sixth and seventh centuries.

Today's Buddhism would not exist without all the efforts of the four mentioned, especially Jian Zheng (Ganjin in Japanese), which was designed to teach and guide Japanese Buddhist monks and stabilize Japanese

Buddhism in its early days. I tried to go to Japan six times. However, the first five attempts failed due to political causes and storms. He lost his sight during the storm that occurred on his fifth attempt. When he tried to go to Japan, he was sixty-six years old. He did not give up a trip to Japan because of the spread of Buddhism. In the end, 753 done. Vol. His contribution to Japanese Buddhism is invaluable.

The Essentials of Buddhism

An argument in the sense of the essence of Buddhism is something that can take many volumes to cover. This is due to the great complexity associated with the religion of Buddhism. However, there is also some irony. Specifically, Buddhism is a very basic religion. This is primarily a cult practice that involves observing simple logic and common sense. This is a far cry from many past world religions that are rooted in spiritualism, mysticism, and magic. No, the main components of Buddhism are more rooted in the core of the individual. This can be considered the basic essence of religion; you are looking for what is inside you, not what makes it exist on the outer plain.

Although there are many different sects of Buddhism, there is a certain common thread that can be found among all. In particular, the goal of Buddhism is to achieve enlightenment. It may be the same goal for everyone, but the path will be different for each person. But what exactly is lighting, and how can it be achieved? The answer brings us back to understanding the basic elements of Buddhism.

Simply put, enlightenment refers to a person who proceeds from a clear understanding of what the true teaching of the Buddha actually means. So, what is the remote meaning of the Buddha's teachings? Well, if you don't enter the stage of enlightenment, something that few people are capable of you can't effectively give an answer. But it would be wrong to assume that spiritual or intellectual relationships will be the root of enlightenment. On the contrary, it would be a transformation that a person would undergo the basis of living in harmony with the concepts of the Buddha. Such steps can only be taken if the basic essential elements of Buddhism are understood.

At the heart of a Buddhist's life is an understanding of the four Nobel truths of life. Understanding these truths will help make life less complicated because they are there...truth. Without contradicting or rejecting the truth, one can gain the advantages of the precept of Buddhist theory. The four Nobel truths represent the idea that life suffers; suffering comes from attachment; when you move away from attachment, you can put an end to your suffering; and you should follow the path of the Buddha to enlightenment. Although the last truth may be ambiguous, the other three truths are obvious. That is, life is never perfect, and there will always be problems that you will have to face. How to deal with these issues will greatly affect whether you get the most out of life. And if you want to avoid suffering in life, it is better never to look at external things for your happiness. This is because such elements only lead to conflict and the development of bad goals in life.

As for the life of a Buddha, there is an eightfold path that must be followed. The eightfold path can be considered cautious because it warns about what to avoid in life, even if it presents the concept in a positive way. The eightfold path will help you achieve the wisdom necessary to achieve enlightenment through the appropriate practice of how you should live your life. The eightfold path involves: seeing reality for what it really is; using good intent to develop an ethical life; using correct speech when you speak; you can do the right thing in everything you do; earn the right livelihood and stay away from monetary gain, immorally; always work with the right effort; be aware in a positive way, and always use the right concentration to succeed in your business.

Basically, the essence of Buddhism is to do things in the "right" way. When you perform the actions of your life correctly and morally, you eliminate a lot of problems. You can get more out of life when you are honest and sincere about your potential. This is not a case where you are acting immorally. This is why the concept of karma is so vital to understanding Buddhism.

Karma, as most people understand it, refers to the notion that what you do well in the world comes back to you. If you do immoral or bad things, you will get the same results in return. It is obvious that it would be useful and more reasonable to do good things to others since this will ultimately benefit the person who does the deeds.

Again, actions are not necessarily rooted in anything other than the basic wisdom of common sense. This separates Buddhism from many other practices in world history that were more mystical in their approach. This does not mean that Buddhism transcends these old religions as much as it is rooted in its own unique essential tenants.

Buddhism Symbols

Buddhist culture is known as one of the oldest cultures in the world. There are more than twenty-five centuries. The ideals and ideas of Buddhists have led countless people around the world. Buddhist culture is mainly associated with the knowledge of "Siddhartha Gautama" known as "Buddha." "The names of the two most important branches of Buddhism are Theravada and Mahayana. In ancient times, people did not use Buddha statues for worship. Instead, they chose to symbolize the Buddha.

Some of the main symbols of Buddhism are the imprint of the Buddha, the Stupa, the Wheel of Dharma, and the lotus. As the ideas of Buddhism spread around the world, it also helped Buddhist symbols reach many new and different people.

The most common symbol of Buddhism is the footprint of the Buddha.

According to Buddhists, these footprints of the Buddha symbolize the bodily appearance of the Lord. These paintings were reproduced from ancient stones in Bodhgaya, India. This is the place of Buddha's enlightenment. In this symbol of Buddhism, there are many other symbols such as swastikas, Loti, and Dharma wheels. These tracks exist in many countries such as India, China, Japan, Singapore, and Sri Lanka. According to legend, a Buddhist legend says that after the Buddha attained enlightenment, his foot left an imprint on the stone where he stood.

Another symbol of Buddhism is the Stupa. The main meaning of the Stupa is "crowd."- This is a hilly structure containing remnants of Buddhism. Thus, these stupas are very sacred for such people. These stupas are vital, consisting of five components. Each part has its own meaning and presentation. The Stupa has a square base that symbolizes the earth. The hemispherical part is water. The conical part is a fire. There is a Crescent moon, which is a symbol of air and the point of dissolution, as well as a round disk representing space.

The Lotus wheel and Dharma are other parts of these symbols. The lotus is deeply rooted in the mud, but the flower is open to the sun. It looks very beautiful and fragrant. In Buddhism, the lotus represents the true nature of beings returning through "Samsara" ("Samsara" - the process of determining the cycles of birth, death, and rebirth in Buddhism and Hinduism) for the simplicity and splendor of enlightenment. The Dharma wheel contains eight spokes. They are an eight-week journey. According to tradition, it symbolizes the rotation of the Buddha with the wheel of law or reality.

Some other important symbols of Buddhism have different colors. Special five colors-white, yellow, red, blue, and green. Like white, it is believed to include extreme cold, such as snow, quality, or very burning quality, such as flaming metal. Both can be life-threatening, as well as a reminder of grief with the ends of things. It also embodies purity, sanctity, and purity. In addition, it also tells us to go beyond the darkness of slavery. These colors symbolize the mood. It is believed that spiritual transformations can be achieved by meditating on these different colors.

Buddhism Symbol

The symbol of Buddhism is an integral and important part of the Buddhist religion. The symbol of Buddhism reflects the teachings of Lord Gautama, the Buddha, that he himself is enlightened character. Buddhist religion has never used an image or statue of a Buddha, but a symbol as part of its religious rites. But today, Buddhist rituals and ceremonies are incomplete without the statue/image of the Lord Buddha, and his important stands in any type of Buddhist ceremony. However, this does not mean that the symbol of Buddhism in the modern world of great importance, far from it, these symbols still occupy the central place in its ceremonies and rites.

The symbol of Buddhism consists of eight symbols, which are very important for the disciple of this particular religion. Passionate followers of Buddhism know the importance and significance of these symbols within the framework of the teachings of Lord Gautama Buddha. These eight symbols are popular representations, followed by followers of Buddhism with great devotion. It is relevant, hundreds of years, and just as important today.

Eight Buddhist symbols that are revered and held with great respect from his disciples have meanings, which mean for each Buddhist. These symbols are infinite knot, goldfish, Lotus, Om mani Padme hum, parasol, swastika, Triratna, and Varada Mudra. These symbols are especially important in Theravada Buddhist countries such as Sri Lanka and Thailand. With the spread of religion, its symbolism was enriched by different cultures of individual areas. If you look at Buddhism in Tibet, it has a rich symbolic tradition. Eight auspicious symbols arealso known as Ashtamangala (Ashta meaning eight and Mangala meaning auspicious) in Sanskrit.

The symbol of Buddhism has a meaning that enriches and stimulates. Here is a short of what the symbols:

    A. Parasol (chattra) - royal and spiritual power
    B. Goldfish (suvarnamatsya) - good luck, fertility, and salvation
    C. Treasure Pot (kalasha) - spiritual and material abundance
    D. Lotus (padma) - mental and spiritual purity
    E. Shell (sankha) - the glory of Buddha's teachings
    F. Infinite knot (Shrivastava) - the infinite wisdom of the Buddha

G. The winning flag (dhvaja) - the victory of the Buddha's teachings and wisdom over ignorance

H. Wheel (dharmachakra) - the teachings of the Buddha.

The symbol of Buddhism also includes color. There are five colors of white, yellow, red, blue and green, and symbolic gestures called mudra. The adherents of Buddhism use these eight auspicious symbols on prayer flags, integrated mandalach and thangkach, and used in other forms of ritual art. The wheel of life is another important symbol for Buddhists. The symbol represents a universe understood by Buddhists. Therefore, eight symbols and five colors are important for Buddhists, such as Lord Gautama Buddha.

The Significance of the Lotus Symbol in Buddhism

There are eight auspicious symbols in Buddhist art, and the lotus flower is one of the most important. In fact, one could credibly state that the lotus flower is the best known of all symbols. It is often described in works of art because of its deep connection with the notion of enlightenment, which is the primary purpose of the practice of Buddhism.

The lotus flower and its Lotus-derived position in the practice of Buddhism have a higher level of complexity than most realize. This is because the flower has a deep symbolic meaning far beyond the appearance of the flower or the assumption that all religions need an icon. The lotus flower was not selected to simply play an iconic role. However, the presence of the lotus is vital because of the lotus position; an essential component in the worship of Buddhism plays such an important role in the practice of Buddhism.

The lotus position in the practice of Buddhism is something that is often misunderstood by those who do not understand what the position is designed to promote. For some, the lotus position seems "cool" and is good enough for them to use it in their meditative practice. However, there is more to the position than mere appearances. When we are of the mind that the position is valid on the basis of an opinion of superficial value, we run the risk of being able to reject it just as well. And honestly, it is better not to refuse any element of Buddhist practice, not to mention such an important element as the lotus position and its symbolism.

The key to understanding the lotus is to have a deeper understanding of what it implies. In Buddhism, there are additional intricacies in examining symbolism in any image. This is because Buddhism promotes notions of duality and open interpretations. Since Buddhism is rooted in what already exists in the self, it is common that interpretations of symbols are not clearly defined.

This does not mean that there is no order to the symbolism found in Buddhism. Such an approach would be chaotic and sloppy; these are certainly two components far from what Buddhism represents. So, there are general characteristics that the lotus flower represents.

The selection of the lotus flower in Buddhism stems from the fact that it is a flower that is able to bloom while simultaneously throwing its seeds.

This is very related to the components of Buddhist Karma since Karma revolves around cause and effect. In some cases, there may be similarities between cause and effect, and other scenarios may lead to the exact opposite reaction to what you originally expected. The key here is that you have to understand that karma will turn out to be a salvation or a loss depending on your approach to life.

Lotus flowers are also known to float on water. In some cases, water can be Virgin and clear. In other cases, water can be polluted or otherwise dirty. The symbolism of this should be considered quite obvious. The fact that the meditative position is based on the lotus flower is not clearly selected without clear deliberation.

Water dirt can represent evil, dangers, and the darkest side of life. The lotus flower rises above and floats on such ugliness. The concept of meditation in the lotus position presents the idea that a person can rise above such complexities and difficulties and maintain his composure and correct mood. Of course, you can also maintain such a calm in all environments, whether it is the central theme of Buddhists, practice a calm mind that coexists in all environments.

The lotus flower floats not only on dirty, cloudy water. He was born of vile and dirty mud, but you would not know it by looking at such a beautiful flower. Whatever dirt it comes from, the true nature of the lotus flower emerges from its dark origins and rises above it. One could consider this as the ultimate form of enlightenment, which probably explains why the lotus is so often reflected in Buddhist symbolism and works of art.

One could say that the real heart and essence of a human being lie in the symbolism of the lotus. Given the brilliance of the flower and what it represents, it is understandable that the images of the lotus turned out to be so memorable over the centuries.

Why Christians Practice Buddhism

Thomas Merton, a well-known Catholic monk, belonging to the Trappist tradition of standing (the Cistercian order of strict respect), once said that he wanted to "become as good a Buddhist as possible."

Before turning to Catholicism between the ages of twenty and thirty, he read about Christian mysticism. He read works such as the confessions of Augustine and Thomas Kempis' imitation of Christ, and other books that unconsciously relate to him the taste of God's experience directly through the process of negation.

After he was ordained as a monk, Merton was only interested in Catholicism for many years, and nothing else, but gradually, growing up, and after reading authors such as Saint John the cross and Meister Eckhart, began to become more and more interested in mysticism or in the direct experience of God.

Merton then began to understand the universal nature of mysticism and that Buddhism, in particular, faced mysticism more clearly than Christianity about how to understand it, and especially provided a non-religious method for making fundamental changes in its life. This attracted him to Zen and was eventually written by Zen and the birds of appetite with DT Suzuki, which unambiguously explained the similarities between Buddhism and Christianity on deeper mystical levels. Merton began to explore universal spiritual truth in the structure of his Catholic faith.

For some, Buddhism has become an organized religion, like any other religion, with beliefs, ceremonies, and rituals. However, the original Buddhism, as the Buddha learned, was about personal transformation, not religion.

This is what makes fundamental Buddhism compatible with other religions; that there are no requirements of faith. It is completely empirical and is directly connected with the life and problems of life. It confronts the reality that we all experience stress and answers all questions related to stress. Buddhism also sets up a logical plan to end this stress forever.

If only Buddhism could be called a philosophy of how to live your life from day-to-day. This explains why just trying to be good doesn't work without understanding good and evil, and our basic self. We crush our resolve to change, but it never works, and we also meet our old times and again when things get tough.

Buddhism can also be called psychology, because it delves into the realms of the mind to the deeper levels of modern psychology, which deals only with surface irregularities, never comes to the root.

Buddhism can also be called a religion because it explains the experience of the afterlife but is neutral, which does not mean God the Creator or the need for worship or faith. Things become obvious when practicing Buddhism, and the Buddhist practice itself is non-confessional compared to the non-religious beliefs it represents. Buddha once said: "don't believe anything if you can't prove it for yourself."

And a great scientist, Einstein, once said, "the religion of the future will be a cosmic religion. He must transcend the personal God and avoid dogmas and theology. Embracing both the natural and the spiritual, it must be based on a religious feeling that arises from the experience of all, natural and spiritual, and significant unity. In Buddhism, it corresponds to this description. If there is a religion that meets modern scientific needs, it will be Buddhism."

Therefore, according to Einstein and the Buddha, we should not be afraid that Buddhism will compete with his beliefs, because it is not so. Gandhi said a very wise thing; that you can find the deepest roots of your religion by observing other religions, and then return to your faith with new eyes.

The Branches of Buddhism

Like any other religion in the world, Buddhism has several sects with different beliefs and practices. We will start with the most popular border of Buddhism, known as Mahayana. "Mahayana" is the name given to the movement, which can be considered at different stages as a philosophical school, sects, and churches. Although it is not always easy to define its attitude towards other schools and the seven, it certainly became an important aspect of Buddhism in India at the beginning of a new era, in addition to achieving long triumphs in the Far East. The word means a great guide or crew, that is, a rescue vehicle, and opposes Hinayana, a small guide, a name given to the Conservative Party itself, although it was not voluntarily adopted by them.

The simplest description of these two schemes is given by the Chinese passenger I - Jing (635-713 AD), who saw them as a living reality in India. He says, "those who worship Bodhisattvas and recite the Mahayana Sutra are called Mahayanists, and those who do not are called Kinayans. In other words, the Mahajans have their own scriptures that are not included in the Hinayana Canon and worship superhuman beings at a stage of existence just below the Buddha's state and are practically slightly different from Indian deities.

Many functions can be added to the description of I-Ching, but they may not be universal for Mahayana or completely absent in the Hinayana, because no matter how different these two drivers when they were geographically separated, for example, from Ceylon and Japan, it is clear that when they touch each other, like India and China, the difference has not always been dramatic. But on the whole, Mahayana was more popular, but not in the sense that it was easier because some parts of her teaching were extremely designed, but in the sense that she was trying to invent or incorporate teachings acceptable to the masses.

She was less monastic than older Buddhism and more emotional, warmer in Grace, more personal in devotion, richer in art, literature, and rituals, more prone to evolution and development, while Hinayana was conservative and harsh, isolated in her monasteries and open to plausible but unjust accusations of selfishness.

While European writers generally speak of two guides or Yang-large and small-and, although this is obviously an important distinction for historical purposes, Buddhists, Hindus, and Chinese do not list the three most common. It is Zravakayana, the guide of the ordinary bhikshu who hopes to become Arhat, Pratiekabuddhayana for the rare beings able to become Buddha, but not preach the law to others, but unlike the Mahayana, or the guide of the Buddha and Bodhisattva.

As a rule, these three vehicles are not considered hostile or even incompatible. Thus, in the Lotus Sutra, he claims that there is, in fact, only one conductor, and although he wisely succumbed to human weakness, the Buddha clearly indicates that there are three conductors for every taste. And the Mahayana is not a single car, but a train consisting of different cars from different classes. It has a clear next step, known in Sanskrit as Mantra and Vajrayana, but generally described by Europeans as Tantrism. This stage adopted certain traits of Hinduism, such as spells, spells, and Goddess worship, and incorporated them into Buddhism.

The Different Sects of Buddhism

We have a record of Indian thought for about 3000 years. It hits directly from distant points like Balkh, Java, and Japan and is still alive and active. But life and action mean change, and such an extension in time and space implies variety. We are talking about converting foreign countries, but the religion that is transplanted also undergoes conversion. Otherwise, it cannot enter new brains and hearts. Buddhism in Ceylon and Japan, Christianity in Scotland, and Russia are not the same, although they profess to worship the same teachers. It is easy to discuss on the other side, but this can only be done by putting aside non-essential differences of great practical importance.

Westerners are quite willing to admit that Buddhism is changeable and easily corrupted, but it is not unique in this sense. I doubt that Lhasa and Tantrism are altogether more of the teaching of the Buddha than of the papacy, the Inquisition, and the religion of the Emperor of Germany, the teaching of Christ.

A religion is the expression of thought of a particular age and cannot really be permanent in other times, other thoughts. The apparent permanence of Christianity is due, first, to the suppression of many original teachings, such as Christ, turning the cheek to the drummer and Paul's belief in the near end of the world, and, secondly, the adoption of new social ideals that have no place in the New Testament, such as the abolition of slavery and the abolition of slavery.

The Buddhism of Brahmanism suggests a comparison with the Christianity of Judaism, but the comparison breaks down in most points of detail. But there is a real similarity, namely that Buddhism and Christianity both won their greatest triumphs outside the land of their birth. Spirit flowers, if they can be transplanted, often bloom with special vigor on foreign soils.

Is Buddhism a Religion or a Philosophy?

Buddhism is considered one of the world's leading Religions, with about 350 million followers, mainly in Asia, but it also became popular in Western countries in the last century. However, looking at Buddhism from a western point of view, many people argue that it is more a philosophy than a religion, because it lacks some of the qualities of others, especially theistic Religions. Even among practicing Buddhists, there are serious disagreements on this issue. Is Buddhism a religion, philosophy, or something completely different?

If we look at how Buddhism is practiced in most Asian countries, many features of religion can be found. People practice religious rituals and practices, such as providing flowers and incense as Buddha substrates. In addition, some forms of Buddhism that are very popular in Asian countries are very similar to theistic Religions, such as the respect of the Amitabha Buddha in Pure Earth Buddhism or Avalokiteshwara in many Buddhist schools.

However, the oral teachings of the historical Buddha Siddhartha Gautama, transmitted by the Sutra of the Palian Canon, paint a completely different picture of Buddhism:

In the Kalama Sutra (Anguttara Nikaya 18:9), The Buddha teaches that he should not rely on the traditions, rumors, letters, or authority of his teachers. Thus, he opposes blind faith, dogmatism, and beliefs that arise from pious reasoning. On the contrary, it is only when a person personally knows that a certain teaching is skillful, impeccable, praiseworthy and conducive to happiness, and is praised by the wise, that he must accept it as a true and practicing one. In short, the Buddha resisted dogmatism and independent thinking based on direct experience.

Some days the Buddha shows an anti-rebalist position, demonstrating the futility of religious rituals. He often reinterpreted the common ritual in his time to draw a moral Conclusion. For example, in Digha Nykae 31, the Buddha adopted a ritual in which a person worshiped in all six directions (four geographical directions, top, and bottom)and interpreted it as six different types of harmonious and moral relationships (parents, teachers, spouses, friends/colleagues, servants and ascetics and priests).

From this brief overview of Buddhist teachings and the attitude of the Buddha towards blind faith, dogma, and rituals, it can be concluded that Buddhism is more a philosophy than a religion. But is it really?

In the parable of the poisoned arrow (Majjhima Nikaya 16), The Monk continues to ask the Buddha philosophical questions about the origin and infinity of the world, about himself, or about awakening. Buddha kept silent on these questions, saying that the answer to these questions was useless and did not stop the suffering as if the person had been injured by a poisoned arrow, instead of letting the doctor pull the arrow, she continued to ask questions about the arrow or arrow that dropped the arrow. Therefore, the Buddha opposed a philosophy that has only theoretical value and a teaching that solves the most important problem of suffering (Dukha).

Instead of religious rituals or Theoretical Philosophy, Buddha taught three basic principles:

Strength is the morality expressed in Buddhist Commandments

Samadhi-concentration and mental discipline obtained by the practice of meditation

Panna-wisdom and understanding that leads to the end of suffering

In this regard, although Buddhism does not share many features of other Religions, Buddhism can be considered a religion in the truest sense of the word, because it leads to salvation, that is, to the end of suffering, to a state called Nirvana.

Beyond the Happiness: Buddhism Viewpoint

Many people tried to define their own happiness and be happy. The truth is that there is no single definition of happiness because each of us has different desires, goals, interests, and values. Therefore, it is very important for each of us to develop his definition of happiness. In this way, you can finally seek happiness in your life.

However, determining our happiness is a very difficult task due not only to the complexity of happiness itself but also to our sense of spiritual materialism. Because spiritual materialism is rooted in our minds, we tend to deceive ourselves in the materialistic sense of happiness unconsciously. First of all, what makes things worse is that our penchant for mysticism, idolatry, and exclusivity. As a result, many people may not yet be able to be truly happy.

Buddhists are no exception to materialistic feelings of happiness. In fact, Buddhism in Japan has developed various philosophies and practices based on spiritual materialism. For example, the famous Vajrayana Buddhism (Shingon Mikkyo) developed its secret Bible and practiced mainly to treat diseases and protect Japan from external diseases. Pure earthly Buddhism (Jodo Shu) developed a "simple practice," suggesting that man completely saved the Buddha as soon as the man whispered this or that phrase in the Buddhist Bible. The pure earth brought Buddha the pure certainty that she had been saved or happy without self-improvement. Hard Zen Buddhism used Zen meditation as almost the only fully enlightened practice, while ancient Buddhism simply used meditation to create the opportunity to allow one's consciousness to experience Nirvana. When you focus on reinventing the notion of happiness in Japanese Buddhism beyond ancient Buddhism and ordinary Bible Buddhism in Japan, you may find that happiness exists because of the existence of unhappiness. Because misfortune usually comes from selfishness (egocentric thinking) and materialism, it is important to be altruistic rather than materialistic, even if we have a body and spirit that usually suffers more than selfishness and materialism. Some Buddhists believe that the altruist, and not the materialist, is a state of happiness. However, taking away our unhappiness does not mean that we are happy because there is no happiness without unhappiness. This is what the

Buddha faces as a challenge. After all, Buddha defined it as "empty" which means perfect altruism or harmony in the world. Therefore, the Buddha had another task to determine the conditions outside of happiness because there was no more luck in the void. According to Buddha, this state is called Nirvana when eternity exists in an ideal world.

Answering Your Buddhism Questions

If you look closely at history, you will see that religion has influenced most historical events. It can be a conquering nation that has one religion and wants to spread its beliefs. Over the past two thousand years, Christianity has become one of the most popular religious directions. But not the most popular. Do you know what is the most popular religion/spiritualism in the world? It's Buddhism. This unique lifestyle and religion have roots in the depths of centuries and have hundreds of millions of followers.

This is a spiritual journey into Nirvana, which encourages practitioners to lead a faithful life and do what is considered right. There are even many people who practice parts of Buddhism that are by no means Buddhist. Yoga is a very popular activity, but it comes from this spirituality. In this book, we will look at the basics of this spirituality and religion. I hope this will shed light on a culture that has gained popularity in Western civilizations.

When did Buddhism originate?

It is difficult to answer this question. Some people believe that the beginning of Buddhism occurred when the Buddha was born. Others believe that the beginning was when he really achieved enlightenment and began to teach his followers. If you hold the opinion that it started with his birth, then it would date around the year 556 B.C.

If we follow the belief that it began with its enlightenment, then it dates back around 531 BC. As you can see, this is a very old religion that dates back long before many modern religions. This story is an exciting mixture of fantasy. Like many well-known spiritual leaders who are found in religions around the world, Buddha is said to communicate with the gods.

How can she become a Buddhist?

Becoming a Buddhist is not the right or wrong way. Usually, most people get acquainted with Buddhism through friends or relatives. It is perfectly normal to ask questions when faced with a faith that is completely different from the one you had in childhood. Knowledge is essential for understanding this spiritual way of life.

You can declare a Buddhist, but if you don't know about the practices and philosophy, you're just a shadow of what is actually a Buddhist. There are many great resources on the internet and in bookstores. Many Buddhists have local branches and gather together to meditate and talk about their beliefs.

What are some Buddhist concepts?

One of the philosophies that the Buddha firmly believed and talked about often was that nothing in this life is eternal. Everything disappears. He considered that attachment to material goods and status was the fall of man. There are other tenants, such as not to hurt others who are practiced all over the world. Many people believe that this is a pacifist view of life, but it is one that includes Buddhism.

Why is meditation so important in Buddhism?

Meditation is very important for Buddhism. This is the cornerstone of the whole religion or spirituality. Meditation is the way Siddhartha became a Buddha. It was thanks to careful examination of his life and the surrounding world that he realized the true path to happiness or enlightenment. Meditation is the only inhabitant of Buddhism, located in all different sects. The sects may differ according to the correct way or what to indulge in or abstain from, but meditation is the key to finding the answer to death, disease, and happiness.

7 Reasons Why You Should Learn About Buddhism

1. Buddhism is the only great religion in the world that teaches something radically different. Don't learn to worship one God or many gods; they are focused on the problems we have here in this world.

2. It is practiced by about 500 million people: this does not mean that because of the large number of practitioners, it is good or true, but it does mean that they can adapt to different cultures and environments.

3. You can use your philosophy even if you practice a different religion: the basic teachings of Buddhism are compatible with other religions. You can be a Christian and still apply the practical teachings of the Buddha.

4. Faced with problems that affect everyone: the Buddha said that he learned about suffering, its origin, and what to do with it. Everyone in the world is suffering. The Buddha says that you can erase the suffering. Why not listen to it?

5. It can adapt to your situation: you don't need to be a monk or pray 12 hours a day to become a Buddhist, just use the practical teachings of the Buddha in your life.

6. This is a religion: in the West, it is often debated whether Buddhism is a religion or not. It is a religion because, in some of its expressions, it includes rituals and worship. If you are busy, you can become a member of the Buddhist community.

7. This Is not a religion, but a philosophy: some say that Buddhism is not a religion because it does not include God or gods. You can take the basic teachings of the Buddha and apply them as a philosophy of life without becoming a member of a religious group. You will see how practical they are.

Buddhism and Karma

One of the main beliefs of Buddhism is the law of karma. The word karma is a word that is very common in our world. Lately, I have not looked at the dictionary to see if it has entered the speech of vocabulary, but it is certainly the speech of our culture. But what does this mean for Buddhists?

To truly understand this doctrine and what it really means to Buddhists and Hindus, we must first look at a basic premise of Indian religious life. This is the doctrine of reincarnation, known in India as Samsar. Samsara is a cycle of death and rebirth in which every living being is "captured."The word Samsar means "wandering."We are wandering, and we do not know where we come from and where we are going. Indians consider this process burdensome because we have lived and lived millions and millions of lives with no visible end. The purpose of Indian religions is to end this cycle. This is what Buddhism seeks-for Samsara's freedom.

Karma is the law of retribution that governs and governs the Samsar cycle.You probably know what it means to say that someone has bad karma. It means something unfortunate that probably derives from what they did in the past, either in this life or in the previous life.

In India, the word karma only means "action."So bad karma is a bad action. Good karma is a good deed. Thus, the cycle of death and rebirth, the cycle of Samsar, is governed by an invaluable law: What you do now will give a result in future life. You need to find a way to work with this law to address a positive solution to the problem of Samsara.

You might ask when we talk about the law of karma: where can karma lead you? What are the possible areas of the renaissance? You may be born as a god, as a demigod or as a small category of gods, sometimes called demons, as a human being, as a spirit, as an animal or as a spirit in hell. Sometimes people wonder when they feel that hell is an important term in Buddhism or Indian religion in general.

So, you need to work with this law to have a good rebirth in future life. What do you do to have good karma? Do your duty. Each person in India is assigned to a specific group. Perhaps you were born into a princely family. You could be a Brahmin. Each group has its own responsibilities. If you do what you have to do, you will have a good degeneration.

But is this the solution to the problem of Samsara? Buddhists say no. They have a different approach to this problem. Samsara's problem solving is NIRVANA.

Why Buddhism is So Appealing

Buddhism is always considered unique in the religious landscape. We can't find anything like this. What makes it so unique and attractive? Why is popularity currently increasing? Buddhism is a very humane religion (if we could call it that). It deals with the deeply human and common to all problems. What does the Buddha teach? He learns about suffering. Its origin and solution for this. What could be more appealing than putting an end to our suffering?

Siddhartha Gautama is considered the founder of Buddhism. According to tradition, he lived in Northern India for about 500B.C., a Prince, was born. When he was born, some priests told his parents that his son would be a successful man, both as a king and as a religious leader. Siddhartha's father believed that this was the most convenient way to become a great king, so he protected his son and did not allow him to leave the palace.

Siddhartha lived until the age of 29. At this stage of his life, he witnessed suffering for the first time. It was one of the most shocking moments of his life. He saw a sick man, an old man, and a dead body. He realized that this is the fate of every person. This realization was so shocking to him that he decided to spend his life searching for a solution.

First, he became a monk. He joined a group of other ascetics and tried to cope with the problems of old age and death by starving until there was nothing left but skin and bones. It wasn't a particularly pleasant time for him, and it didn't produce the results he wanted. He saw that this was not the way out, so he tried to go the other way.

He retreated from this strict style of saving to practice the average trip. The goal, this time, is to avoid two extremes. One of them is the extreme of self-denial. Too much to deny. Do not worry about the needs of the body and the individual. The second extreme is self-harm. A form of condescension that affects not only how people live, but also how people think. Especially how they think of themselves.

When Siddhartha found the middle way, everything became faster for him. He sat under a tree and thought. In the dark of night, he went through the steps of meditation and finally understood what causes the world to suffer and how it can end forever.

What is true, do you understand? He taught his students that everyone in life suffers. Pretty pessimistic, isn't it? But this was only the beginning. There was hope in his voice. He also gave us permission to suffer. Its solution is not temporary. Its decision is permanent and final. His solution is the only one that works.

This is why Buddhism is so attractive. It faces a problem that is common to all. The problem of suffering. Buddhism says that we can put an end to our suffering.

Why Buddhism is Unique

Some aspects of Buddhism challenge our ideas about the nature of religion itself. I have a definition of religion from an old dictionary that I have loved for years since I was a student. It looks like this: "religion is the service and worship of God or gods in the form of worship."I imagine many of you will define religion using the word "God" somewhere in that definition.

Buddhists really worship the gods. Gods are part of Buddhist life; they are important in some aspects of Buddhist ritual. However, Buddhists deny the existence of a unique Almighty God who created the world. Buddha is the same person as us who faced life's difficulties and developed a human reaction.

When we talk about Buddhism, we have to face the possibility that religion can develop at the deepest level without worrying about God, the Creator. This will trigger our understanding of what a religion is in itself.

On the contrary, Buddhists ask questions like this: what is the highest reality? How do I know?

Another aspect of Buddhism that would be amazing and inspiring for us is related to the nature of ourselves. Many religious traditions emphasize the importance of the immortal soul. In Buddhism, this is not the case. Buddhists say that there are human personalities, few, like the river. It flows constantly. It can also be like a constant fire. The soul itself is not eternal, not eternal. This is part of a variable process.

The idea of an immortal soul is just an illusion that we impose onour psychological and emotional needs. Buddhist ideas about ourselves encourage us to take a fresh look at some fundamental questions that belong to us all as human beings: who am I? How can I unlock my human potential?

The Most Important Teaching of Buddhism

One of the most important Buddhist teachings is the concept of not-self. Buddhists insist that there is no permanent identity that lasts at any time. What do they mean when they say there's no "I"?

In traditional Buddhism, this means that there simply is no permanent identity that lasts at any given time. If there is no constant identity, what does this phenomenon that we associate with our physical and cognitive presence in this world? The answer to this question in the classical Buddhist doctrine is five aggregates. These are the five things that lead from a material form to a set of consciousness.

These five aggregates are short-term, but they combine into bundles to give us the illusion of some sort of longevity, like the flow of a river or the flame of a candle. Buddhists think of identity as a constant flow, the flow of a phenomenon that transforms into a moment.

The classic question that calls into question the discussion about the nature of oneself is this: if there is no "self" what is born again? The classic answer to this question is the flow of consciousness itself. When a death occurs in this world, and bundles of aggregates that make up the personality, begin to scarce, the last moment of consciousness creates another moment of consciousness in other places, which begin to form as a new identity. It's not the same, and it's no different from a pre-existing personality, it's just a causal relationship that leads from one moment to the next.

Because of the causal continuity between one moment and the other, one can say that they are the same person at the moment. However, when we look closely at our personalities, we realize that every moment changes and the idea that one moment is equal to the other is nothing more than an illusion.

Buddhism For Beginners Or an Introduction Into the Way of Life

The Buddhist religion is based on helping people overcome the suffering and uncertainty of human survival by canceling desire and ego. Buddhists call this result a state of Nirvana or peace of mind. Religion itself is tolerant, but, on the other hand, criticism or suggestions of reform are not accepted. The belief system focuses on meditation. Much of the long life of Buddhist monks goes to show how useful meditation and yoga are. The essence of this religion is that life is full of suffering (although you may doubt this when you look at famous Buddhists like the Dalai Lama). The most precious thing in the Buddhist religion is life after death, and it does play an important role in this religion.

The roots of Buddhism

Buddhism was founded by Siddhartha Gautama, who lived and died 563 years later and 483. before the birth of Christ. Since then, Buddhism and its belief system have spread around the world, and the region where it is most popular is, of course, Asia. This is consistent with the moral teachings of other religions but goes beyond providing a long-term goal in our existence, through wisdom and true understanding. Being a Buddhist does not mean believing in a God or gods, if you like it. It is often compared to Christianity on a theme that emphasizes caring for its neighbor eight times. His birth was in India (since Buddha was an Indian Prince), and Buddhism grew out of the great traditions that Hinduism brought. The religion began in India but spread from there to many parts of Asia. Buddhist practices vary widely in different parts of the world and have become very popular these days. In addition to celebrities like Richard Gere, who practice active Buddhism, there are also countless monks and nuns. A Buddhist monk or Buddhist nun sometimes lives as emigrants, and sometimes lives in communities. These monks and nuns - in addition to the spiritual and practical advice of their community often study teachings about death and rebirth that are not easy to understand.

Who was the Buddha?

The Buddha was an Indian Prince and, as mentioned earlier, was called Buddha Siddhartha Gautam and lived between 563-483 BC. He accepted the main Hindu doctrines of reincarnation and karma, and also implemented it in Buddhism. The Buddha told his followers and forbade them to worship him, but at that time, he was depicted (and other Holy beings) like compassionate gods. He also spoke about his movement on how to start the wheel of religion. The founder said that "I" and the world around me are not real. He refused to discuss topics such as the science of the soul, the creation of the universe, and the existence of God, and this formed a large part of his life.

Meditation is an important part of Buddhist life

Meditation allows us to develop these moods that promote our peace and well-being and help us root out those who don't. This is a great way to relax and release the tension of the day flowing out of our body. This is done in order to enjoy the ritualized songs and lifestyle practices offered by the Buddhist religion. This can be Buddhist art, meditation, visiting a Zen garden, or even yoga, which helps us in a meditative state. Speaking of meditation as an important part of Buddhist life, the art of meditative practice is something we all need to learn.

Spiritualism

For some, Buddhism is a simple religion, but for others, it is a spiritual journey to be something else. Being one of these Buddhists requires a life dedicated to hard spiritual work. Only those who are initiated can hope to reach this stage of Nirvana, although this includes not only monks and nuns. These Buddhist monks tend to be more committed to spiritual development, shave their heads, only wear three clothes, and own only some essential items. The monks are responsible and are in constant contact with the local people and advise them in a secular and spiritual way. It is very important for Buddhists to know that even the wisest and devoted disciples of the Buddha do not know his spiritual thought in all aspects. A person cannot escape his spiritual nature, and if he runs away from the true God, thousands of liars are ready to close him; this is one of the Proverbs of the Buddhist worlds.

Suffering in Buddhism

The traditional summary of the Buddha's teachings is given in four categories, the so-called Four Noble Truths.

* The truth of suffering (Dukkha)

* The aspect of suffering (Samudaya)

* Cessation of suffering (Nirodha)

* The truth of the path (Mrga) that leads to the end of suffering.

Some say that if you understand the truth of suffering, you implicitly understand all four Noble Truths.

The truth of suffering is expressed in the simple statement that everything is suffering. This phrase, the first doctrinal hypothesis to be discussed, presents us with a problem. This is not easy to interpret.

If you know Buddhist people, if you are a Buddhist person, you know that the Buddhist tradition is not full of sadness. This is not a depressing tradition. In many ways, it has a certain lightness.

Buddhism is light, wavering, easy. It floats almost like a religious tradition through the complexity of this world. The basic statement in the Four Noble Truths, the statement that everything suffers, poses an interpretive dilemma.

How does the statement that everything suffers, the buoyancy and lightness of the Buddhist experience come from this statement?

The first way to begin answering this question is to note that the ancient tradition of Buddhist teaching interprets the expression "everything suffers" in three separate ways. Everything suffers in one or more of the following three ways.

Three types of suffering

The first of these types of suffering is called dukkha-dukkha. Suffering is suffering. Obvious suffering in situations where things cause physical or mental pain.

The second type of suffering is called viparinama-dukkha. Suffering from transformation or change. This means that even the most pleasant things can cause suffering when they start to change and disappear.

The third type of suffering is Sankhara-dukkha. Suffering from conditional States. This category of dukkha is associated with pleasant things that can cause pain even in the midst of pleasure, if this pleasure is based on an illusion about the nature of the object or even the nature of the self.

When I talk about these three types of suffering, I try to illustrate them by constructing a parable that may seem modern, but I think it is related to Buddhist examples that are often used to explain the nature of suffering.

This is the parable of the machine. I'm trying to imagine scenarios in which a car can cause some form of suffering. First of all, you have a guy in a car driving down the road, sees his girlfriend on the sidewalk, calls her, and runs in the back of the bus.

There is a huge accident, and what he hears is dukkha-dukkha. The palpable physical suffering of a car accident. This is easy to understand.

The second type of suffering comes if you are tied to this machine. Many people relate to this. They have cars that they like. They don't have a good time in the winter. Winter is cruel. There's a lot of ice. People vandalize cars. Rust slides over some parts of the car, and the front end becomes unbalanced.

As you can see, the machine is beginning to disintegrate. It makes you suffer in relation to the pleasure, the attachment that you have invested in this object when it starts to run away from you.

This is also pretty clear. Viparinama-dukkha, the suffering that comes from change, is a fairly simple concept to understand.

The third concept is a little more complex. And I'm not sure that most of the time I can really convey it in this example. The way I do it is to imagine someone in a car, fully invested, with all their ego in this powerful object. He roared up and down the Boulevard, feeling the pleasure and energy of being in this powerful embodiment of his masculinity.

And ask yourself if he is really happy now. If you ask him if he is happy, of course, he will say Yes. The pleasure of this experience is extremely satisfying. This cannot be denied. It is a physical and emotional feeling that provides reality in its own right. But is this real happiness?

I think we know enough about situations like this in our world to start wondering if this is where satisfaction really comes from. Partly because it is based on some kind of illusion about the nature of the object, and illusions about the nature of the individual, and how your ego can be embedded in a physical object like this, that arise and disappear.

Sometimes, in certain situations, perhaps in many situations, we suffer in ways we are not aware of, because of the illusions we have about the nature of our self or the nature of the objects that inhabit our world.

Death and Buddhism

Acceptance of death in the Buddhist tradition

The notion of death is something with which we, as human beings, have always struggled to reach an agreement. In our Western culture, we live by denying the simple fact that we will all die one day. In this materialistic world, where consumerism has become a religion, trying to achieve happiness by accumulating earthly goods leaves us completely unprepared for the approach of the end.

When this happens, our society constantly invents new words to distract us from the reality of this experience. For example, a person is no longer called a gravedigger but is called a funeral director. The word "coffin" was replaced by the word "coffin" and the funeral turned into a memorial service. Unfortunately, hiding behind words of affection, we do not get rid of this problem, avoiding this painful subject for life as we reach the end of our journey, we are not ready and are afraid to plunge into the unknown. It also makes us feel hopelessly inadequate and unable to cope when someone next to us is mortally ill.

On the contrary, Tibetan Buddhism teaches very early that any life experience is only temporary, and death is inevitable. We learn that the moment of our death is uncertain, that our life is fragile like a burning flame and that the distance between this life and the next is only a few breaths. Even with the support of our loved ones, we will have to face death alone, knowing that no money, wealth or material property will affect the final result. And our closest friends will not be able to prevent it or come with us. It is believed that if we do not accept these basic principles of life, we will not achieve lasting happiness.

To get rid of this fear of the unknown, we must regularly train ourselves to die so that in due course, we are ready. According to the saying, "die before you die, and you never die" in Tibetan culture, monks and nuns practice daily meditation of death. Oriental practitioners learn to pack their supplies every night as if it were their last night in life. Every morning they wake up to live an extra day lived as a bonus to enjoy to the fullest. Although for a Western man, such an obsession with death may seem painful. On the contrary, to be freed from this fear and to accept death as an integral part of the cycle of our existence, especially if we believe that we will be reborn in another life, is to be freed.

Then why are we so afraid of death?

Buddhism teaches us that the greatest cause of our misfortune is attachment. When we learn to let go, we become free. Everything in life is fickle, so we need to enjoy it while it lasts, and then move on. Instead, we cling to temporary material, sensual or emotional pleasures, claiming that they will last forever, so we will inevitably be disappointed when this does not happen. Often people close to death come out of this more spiritual experience. They tell how they learned to love every moment of their lives. Buddhism believes that there are only two important moments when we reach our last breath: what we have done in our lives and the mood in which we find ourselves at the time of our death. That is why it is so important to prepare for this transition. The purpose of spiritual practice is not to feel fear or regret during our death. It is believed that our mental attitude when we breathe the last breath will determine what our next life will be. With meditation, the moment of death can become an amazing spiritual experience, where often comes the moment of great liberation.

This explains why suicide is considered such a tragic act in Buddhism. The act of killing a self does not stop human suffering. Those who die in a depressed and negative state will be reborn in a lower form of life, where their sufferings will be extended. The physical atmosphere and spiritual attitude of those who are present at the time of someone's death are considered very important in helping the patient on his next trip. Thus, meditation sessions that project feelings of comfort, peace, love, and acceptance will be more beneficial for the patient than tears, suffering, and emotional bursts.

In Tibet, it is traditional to read the "Tibetan Book of death" for several days at the bedside of the deceased in order to guide a person through six different bards of transition (intermediaries) between an existence. It is said that the first three phases occur when a person is still alive, and the last three phases occur between the time of death and rebirth in another life.

Accepting this new concept and freeing ourselves from fear will probably be the most liberating experience we have experienced in our lives.

Michael Luck

Taoism

For beginners

A Complete Guide to Discover the Secrets of Taoism Religion and Taoist Philosophy

Taoism, a traditional Chinese religion dating back to 1800. in 2013, when master Zhang Taoling of the Eastern Han Dynasty (25-220) organized a religious Taoist group. Over the years of its development, Taoism has had a profound political, economic, cultural, and ideological impact on ancient Chinese society and is still active.

During the Eastern Han Dynasty, Zhang Taoling moved to mount song Crane (Mount Heming). He claimed to have received a powerful community of Orthodox unity (Zheng Meng Wei) from Supreme Master Lao Tzu and began producing and distributing books promoting the Tao. His teachings focused on the calling of deities, magic and slavery, spirits, and breathing exercises.

During the reign of Wei (220-265 A.D.), The Heavenly Master of Taoism, created by Zhang Taoling, was suppressed and rejected. However, when Zhang Lu and his students moved north of Hanjung, the heavenly master of Taoism began to be reborn in regions where Taoism of the highest level was already practiced. Then it spread throughout the country.

During the period of the Western Yin (265-316 A.D.) and the eastern Yin (317-420 A.D.), some families and influential scholars began to believe in Taoism. Taoism, which began at the grassroots level, has now infiltrated the upper class, and over time has become an integral part of the spiritual life of the ruling class.

So, as more scientists turned to Taoism, the level of Taoist education increased. As a result, a vast set of Taoist scriptures was created that was supposed to provoke Indian Buddhism.

As the Taoist Scriptures spread, three new Taoist sects emerge; the Supreme purity (Shangqing), the divine treasure (Linbao), and the three August sects (Sanhuan).

In 589, the Sui Dynasty (581-618) United China. At that time, several schools of Taoism began the process of integration. Masha's school, which evolved from a cult of high purity, became the dominant school in the south of the country and began to spread to the North. While Buddhism and Taoism practiced during the Sui Dynasty, Taoism developed rapidly, paving the way for this religion to reach its peak during the Tang Dynasty (618-907).

Li Yuan, the founder of the Tang Dynasty, used public faith in Taoism a lot in the struggle to overthrow the Sui Dynasty. When he came to the throne, he announced that Lao Tzu, the founder of Taoism, was his ancestor (the surname is Lao Tzu-Lee, and his name is E.R.). With the exception of Jetian (the only Empress in Chinese history), all emperors worshiped Tang Taoism.

The most influential development of Taoism during the period of the Five Dynasties (907-960) of late Taoism was the rise of the so-called inner alchemy created by Zhongli Quang and Lu Dongby.

Other schools of Taoism were born during the song, Yin, and Yuan dynasties (960-1368 ad). Taoism has entered a new stage of development.

During the Northern Song Dynasty (960-1127 AD), the maoshan school still held a dominant position, and its genre was very clear. The main new schools that emerged during this period were the sects of the heavenly heart (Tiankin) and the Divine Sky (Shenxiao).

In the Southern Song Dynasty (1127-1279), Taoism dominated the seven known as the mascot of the three mountains (Longhu Mountain, Maoshan, and Gezao).

In addition, new sects such as Shenxiao, Donghua, and Zingway were also active during this period.

In addition to the various old and new mascots, there were also pure light sects and Southern lines of the golden elixir of the sect during the Southern Song Dynasty.

The teachings of the supreme unity (Thaya), great Tao (Datao), and complete perfection (Quanzhen) at the end became the main forms of Taoism during the Jin dynasty (1115-1234). The doctrine of the higher unity lasted about 200 years, and at the end of the Yuan dynasty was built in the tradition of the unity of the orthodox (Zhengyi). The Great doctrine of the Tao fell until the end of the yuan era and was also incorporated into the tradition of Orthodox unity. During the Yuan dynasty, perfection and tradition of Orthodox unity became the two main Taoist schools.

After the establishment of the Ming Dynasty (1368-1644 A.D.), Zhu Yuanzhang, the First Emperor of the Ming Dynasty, adopted a policy of use and control of religion to preserve his property as the only dominant force in the country. As a result, Taoism began to fall.

Relatively speaking, the rulers of the Ming Dynasty preferred the tradition of Orthodox unity to the tradition of complete perfection. The first had a higher political status than the second. Zhu Yuanzhang believed that the sole purpose of meditation is practiced a cult full of excellence. It was the same meditation, while the tradition of Orthodox unity maintained human relations and emphasized social customs, which played an important role in social stability. For this reason, he supported the tradition of Orthodox unity.

The rulers of the Qing dynasty (1644-1911 A.D.) believed in Tibetan Buddhism. They knew little about Taoism and therefore do not support or limit its development. The first emperors of the Qing dynasty followed the rulers of the Ming Dynasty and adopted a policy of defending Taoism because of the need to conquer Han China. But after the reign of Qianlong, the Qing rulers began to impose strict control over Taoism, leading to the fall of its political influence and stagnation of Organizational Development.

V. V., between the First Opium War (1840-1842) and the founding of the people's Republic of China in 1949. In the nineteenth century, China experienced a period of political chaos, and the Chinese people suffered so much from the war and lived in great poverty.

Taoist buildings in the famous mountains fell into chaos, and many Taoists left their temples. As a result, Taoism has become closely related to the everyday life of ordinary people. Initially, during the period of the Republic of China to settle in modern society, Taoists tried to imitate the practices of western countries through the creation of national organizations to protect their interests. In 1912, he became one of the best. Anational organization known as the central Taoist Association was founded in Beijing's white cloud temple, with a complete tradition of perfection as a backbone. At the same time, Zhang Yuanku, 23. The heavenly master who founded the Taoist Federation of the Republic of

China in Shanghai, with the tradition of Orthodox unity as the basis. Both organizations were rather poorly organized, and there were no significant events.

After China adopted a policy of reform and openness in 1979, in the XIX century, the Chinese Taoists continued the opening ceremony of the tradition of total perfection and the rules of transferring the mascot of the tradition of Orthodox unity.

In addition, extensive religious activities took place, such as a large ceremonial offering from the sky that surrounds everything. The Chinese Taoist school and Tao faculty in Shanghai to prepare a large number of priests, young and middle-aged; established academic institutes such as the Tao Cultural Research Institute of China and convened several forums in Tao culture; he founded journals such as Chinese Taoism, Daoism, Tao, Taoism, Daoist.

District-level governments approved about 1,500 Taoist monasteries to allow Taoists to participate in religious activities.

There are about 20,000 Taoist inhabitants full of traditions, perfections, and tens of thousands of Taoist priests of traditions of Orthodox unity, as well as countless Taoist students throughout the country. An ancient religion has now turned into a real one. Century with a completely new look.

Ritual

However, this belief in life for the development of the Tao does not belong to Taoist rituals. The rituals of Taoist practice fully correspond to Taoist understanding, but they are influenced by Buddhist and Confucian practices, so they are sometimes quite complex today. Every prayer and charm that is a Taoist ritual or festival must be accurately uttered, and every step of the ritual must be fully observed. A Taoist religious ceremony will be presided over by a Grandmaster (a kind of priest) who supports it, and these celebrations can last from a few days to more than a week. During the ritual, the Grand Master and his assistants must perform all the actions and recitations according to tradition. Otherwise, their efforts are useless. This is an interesting departure from the usual Taoist understanding of "flow tracking" and does not care about external rules or complex religious practices.

Taoist rituals aim to honor the ancestors of a village, community, or city, and the Grandmaster calls the spirits of these ancestor's incense to purify the area. Cleaning is a very important element throughout the ritual. The shared space of everyday life should be transformed into a sacred space for communication with spirits and gods. There are usually four assistants who help the Grandmaster in different titles, whether they are musicians, Saint dancers, or readers. The Grandmaster interprets the text as read by one of his assistants, and this text refers to the elevation of the soul to join the gods and his ancestors. In ancient times, this was a ritual that took place on the stairs leading to the altar to symbolize the ascent of its common environment to the greater ascent of the gods. The ritual can currently be performed on stage or on the floor, and this is heard with the text and actions of the great riding master.

The altar still plays an important role in the ritual, as it is perceived as the place where the earthly Kingdom meets the divine. Taoist families have their own altar where people will pray and respect their ancestors, household spirits, and the spirits of their village. Taoism requires individual worship at home, and rituals and festivals are social events that bring people together but should not be equated with the practice of worshipping other religions, such as going to church or temple. Taoists can adore homes without even attending a festival, and throughout their history, most people have. Festivals are very expensive on stage and are usually funded by members of a town, village, or city. They are usually considered social holidays, but sometimes they are performed when necessary, such as an epidemic or financial struggle. Ghosts and gods are currently attractive for driving the dark spirits that are causing the problem.

Taoism strongly influenced the Chinese culture of the Shang dynasty. The recognition that all things and all people are connected is expressed in the development of art that reflects an understanding of their place in the Universe and their mutual obligations. During the Tang dynasty, Taoism became the state religion during the reign of Emperor Xuanjong, as he believed that it created a harmonious balance in his subjects, and after a while, he was right. The reign of Xuanzong is still considered one of the most prosperous and stable in Chinese history and the culmination of the Tang dynasty.

Taoism has been called state religions several times in Chinese history, and the teachings of the most beloved Confucius (or, sometimes, Buddhism), most likely because of the rituals of those beliefs that provide the Taoist structure, are not enough. Today, Taoism is recognized as one of the largest religions in the world and is still practiced by people in China and around the world.

Is Taoism a Religion?

Often the question of Taoism is whether it is a religion.

The answer you will get depends on who you are talking about.

Taoism was actually practiced as a religion. Around many Taoists. For example, many Southeast Asian Chinese were born Taoists, but not necessarily religious. I'm one of them.

Since it is practiced as a religion, a religious Taoist will give you an affirmative answer.

However, there is something interesting about Taoism as a religion: do not think that when Christ knows Jesus Christ and the Bible, the Taoist, of course, knows Lao Tzu, the founder of Taoism, and his text is more visible by The Tao Te Jing.

The question is, "what do you do as a Taoist?"this can generate a number of responses. The Taoists go to the temples to pray to the gods. But they do not necessarily pray Lao Tseu. They worship deities of religious figures such as Guanyin, historical figures such as Guanyu or legendary figures such as monkeys, which are not necessarily related to Taoism. Lao Tzu, or better known as Taishang Laojun, is only one. And the fans don't care.

In fact, you will be surprised to learn that many religious Taoists do not know Lao Tseu, not to mention the quotes from Tao Jing's poems. They will probably tell you things like respect for the son, personal honesty, and justice, which is a fusion of Chinese culture and not a Lao-Tse thought.

From this point of view, I would consider Taoism or as a reflection of Chinese culture rather than religion.

It is equally interesting that many who read Lao Tzu and speak of Tao are not called Taoists. They teach the Tao Qing to understand the Universe and practice Tao as a way of life. But they do it philosophically, not religiously. There are also those who practice the activities of Tao, meditation, Qigong to Tai-Chi, and who do not even know that the activity is related to Tao.

If you asked these people, is Taoism a religion? We would say that this is not the case.

So, back to the question, is Taoism a religion?

I can conclude that there are two ways to pursue Taoism. One is religious, and the other is not. The religious approach guides

Taoism through religious rituals such as burning joss' wands and giving deities. Non-religious consider this a philosophy and study the teachings of the sages as a way of life.

Among the Chinese, those who consider Taoism as a religion describe Taoism as Tao Jiao (it can be translated by the domain of Tao),and those who consider it as a philosophy describe it as Tao Jia (School of thought of Tao).

Therefore, the answer to the question of whether Taoism is a religion is yes and no.

As a passionate reader gave you Jing, I can not find a book to be religious at all. In fact, it wasn't supposed to be a religious text when it was first written. It was part of the rich intellectual heritage of the Chinese military period around the 4th century B.C.- an era of dynamic, cultural, and intellectual development in ancient China.

Why Is Taoist Tai Chi So Popular?

Taoist Tai Chi is a mixture of Taoism and Tai Chi Chuan. It is a more comprehensive approach than any of them because it works both on your mind and body. It has evolved as a holistic approach to health and well-being and combines both approaches into uniform practice.

Tai Chi Chuan, translated as the ultimate Fist, is a practice developed for defense and its health benefits, so it focuses more on improving the body. Taoist practices are a number of philosophical and religious beliefs that evolved in ancient India and China.

Here's what you need to know.

#1:This practice has its roots in martial arts and Taoism, the set of philosophical traditions and beliefs, which emphasize moderation, compassion, and harmony.

#2: It is a great practice for your mind and body. Her doctors claim that these health benefits:

* Stretching aspects improve the function of ligaments, tendons, and joints.

* It is an exercise in weight and, as such, can help maintain bone density.

* Taoist forms of Tai-Chi stimulate the spinal nerves, which leads to a balanced effect on the nervous system.

* Long stretches reduce muscle tension.

* By relaxing the mind while exercising, the brain requires less energy, and stress levels are reduced.

* Helps regulate the immune system.

#3: Helps you escape the stress of our modern life. For the correct practice of art, it is necessary to calm the mind, which is easier said than in our modern society. You need to move away from worries, doubts, and tasks to your basic nature of peace, compassion, and peace.

Taoist Tai Chi Society is a dynamic nonprofit organization with over 40,000 members in 26 countries. Their task is to bring benefits to everyone. The company is very popular in Canada and is growing rapidly. Some chapters offer courses aimed at recovery for those who have special needs.

If you're serious about improving your overall health, you should definitely try some Taoist Tai Chi exercises. If you feel better and more relaxed, it can be very useful in everyday practice for you. In recent years have been creating many high-quality DVD programs to teach them basic exercises and the philosophy behind the art of Taoist Tai Chi. These programs can help you get started with the basics before looking for professional guidelines.

Chinese Taoist Wisdom for the Modern Day

The Yin/Yang symbol is one of the oldest and most famous symbols in the world, but few people understand its meaning. Although it is widely used in fashion and media, it is actually an ancient Chinese symbol expressing a deep philosophy. It represents two opposite but complementary pillars of existence that exist in everything. Yin represents everything that is feminine, dark, uplifting, receptive and passive, and things that go down and in. Yang is masculine, bright, strong, and expansive, and Moving up.

According to the philosophy, everything contains Yin and Yang, so we see a white spot in the black segment of the Yin/Yang symbols and Vice versa. In fact, when something happens to the extreme, it always happens to its opposite. This is illustrated in nature in many ways, but it applies to all things: a storm precedes and follows a great calm, cold replaces heat, which replaces cold in a constant cycle of seasons; too strict an organization will cause a rebellion when the rules are too strict; a bubble will burst if it is overestimated.

These examples seem trivial, but a person who can see how Yin and Yang work in the world can predict the outcome of an event. Therefore, the ancient Chinese Taoists recognize that everything is constantly changing, moving first in one direction and then in another. Modern Taoists always try to use this principle and, among other things, can help reduce stress without feeling anxious or anxious when obstacles or difficult times, knowing that everything will improve.

- The key is balance. Neither extreme Yin nor extreme Yang is usually very good. In all aspects of life, being between extremes usually makes running smoother and less stressful. For example, someone who is very motivated and always works and is in a hurry is too young and will soon burn out. Again, a teledipendent who never leaves T.V.and has no goals or ambitions is too Yin and may also suffer from poor health and depression. The half between these two extremes is lighter and healthier.

Yin and Yang are used in many Chinese arts and disciplines.

In traditional martial arts and Tai Chi movements, they constantly expand and then come together, and practitioners are encouraged to stay in extreme positions so as not to get out of balance. In Chinese medicine, diseases and medicines are classified as Yin and Yang, and even Chinese cuisine considers these two properties of different foods and tries to balance Yin and Yang in food!

Thus, for the ancient Chinese and those around the world today who adhere to the Taoist discipline, Yin and Yang are not abstract ideas; they are part of the whole world and everything they do. By understanding, looking, and waiting for the influence of Yin and Yang, Taoism can bring a better balance to your life. In these stressful times, these old ideas are as important as they were thousands of years ago, if not more!

A Quick Guide to Taoist Meditation

The daily stress and anxiety you experience at work and in your personal life are many causes of mental and physical stress; this condition can be greatly relieved by practicing the art of Taoist meditation.

Choosing Taoist meditation is a choice for creating, tuning, and directing energy into an orbit in you. When a person reaches this energy, they can use it to improve their life. The energies of the body, emotions, and mind are used to solve problems and achieve a higher level of spirituality. With these advantages, artists will have a more peaceful existence.

Taoist meditation explains two basic principles: Jing and Ding. The first principle, I Ching, is interpreted as peace and silence. Its goal is to move away from external forces in the mental and physical sense and draw all attention to internal self-confidence. Thus, a person is able to control the "five thieves": eyes, ears, nose, tongue, and body. Each of these "thieves "can say goodbye to the inner being with the help of external distractions, "depriving" the person of the ability to control their own energy.

Ding is the second of the two main principles of Taoist meditation. Ding is the concentration and focus of the mind and breath, which, when used in conjunction with the immobility of Jing, since the state is "one-sided consciousness," an emotional state that is not disturbed. This is the goal of striving to practice Taoist meditation.

Along with these two principles, a corresponding breathing technique was achieved. Focusing on the airflow inside and outside the body, working to achieve a soft, smooth, and slow breathing technique requires a little practice. Some find it useful to focus on an object such as a flame to free their inner confidence from all other distractions. Others prefer to simply close their eyes, separating obsessive thoughts from concentration on breathing. Mantras are frequently used in Taoist meditation, were considered focused on the mind for centuries if you are using energy. There are special mantras that are effectively used: "om"- to stabilize the body;"Ah"- to suppress energy, and "drone" which focuses on the mind.

Many people spend a lot of time perfecting the art of Taoist meditation, especially in these tense times of economic uncertainty, when a sense of balance and peace is so needed. While full control of the inner energy and mind requires a lot of practice and time, getting rid of the daily stress and anxiety of everyday life is worth it.

What are the basic principles?

A person is usually a social being who finds meaning more often from his relationships with others and with a higher being.

They say that the goal in which you do something will largely determine how you do it. It is a case of life, purpose, and faith that forces him to live the quality of life that you will have. Taoism is the "path" in life; it provides the meaning of life and the principles that the believer will lead.

Here is a summary of the principles that govern Taoism.

Tao:

Analysts said Tao supports principles compatible with the laws of nature. It's not far from the truth. After all, the principles of Tao describe the path of learning that every person must follow. This principle is also an attempt to answer what, in fact, is the source of the Universe. This is an attempt to explain what is and what is not. This principle says that energy or Q.I.,and its direction of flow determine the state of being, and the Universe, and personality. If you want peace, you must apply this principle of Taoism.

De or Te:

This principle tells how to activate the Tao principle. This emphasizes the need for humility and honesty in the use of the power of Taoism. As a lifestyle de points out that active enforcement of the Tao principle is the only way to exercise their power.

Wu Wei:

In direct translation, Wu Wei refers to "do it effortlessly."That is, as a believer in Taoism, you do not have to force things in your own way. This differs from most principles applied in the West. With regard to these principles, such as capitalism, waiting to use others, and use all your forces to achieve your goal. A Taoist who is not destined to fight for what they do on your way. Instead, we expect to move on to higher forces that will ultimately dominate human events. The ability to give up the power of the Universe leads to a sense of peace.

P U:

This principle of Taoism emphasizes the need to be simple and reconciled with yourself. This principle, which results in an undiluted block, emphasizes the need to have a clear perception of events. So Taoist must take control over events miss of nature, without trying to read more than you see. In this way, the believer is always taught and receives the results of Mother Nature. So, as a believer and an intern, there is never anything good or bad, that's fine.

Taoist Spirituality and Psychotherapy

Lao Tzu and his fine works of Tao Dau Jing (or Tao Dau Jing) guided the ancient Chinese through a chaotic and tumultuous period of political, social, and spiritual crisis during the period of the warring state. Lao Tzu's radical thinking and learning separated from Confucius's study of values, family organization, Good Governance, and social harmony.

The Lao-Tseu study focused on the concept of Wei (leave/leave/no-Action). Wu Wei does not mean that we do not behave or do nothing, but basically teaches us not to force, control, or interfere with ourselves, as well as others. Allowing and without distractions, our mind is motionless and empty, so we act or act as open, flexible, and adaptive as possible.

In my work as a psychotherapist and in my personal experience, I find that this is often our greatest criticism. Our mind constantly and inexorably judges all our feelings, thoughts, and behaviors. Judgments prevent us from living in the present moment and from living fully as we continue to speak in our heads of right or wrong, agreement or disagreement. So, we try to control or limit things and interfere with the natural flow of things, limiting or establishing a barrier against ourselves. Wei's idea can guide us on the path to emotional and psychological health.

I often remind my clients to be kind, not to disturb observers of our thoughts and feelings, and to let everything happen. Our emotional pain and suffering intensify when we ask a question, judge harshly, and try to reject unwanted feelings. Do you have the experience of trying to stop being nervous? And the palms begin to sweat, your heart short, and your face is bright red, and you are more nervous than it should be. By allowing, without being distracted or needing changes, we can perform or act more naturally and adaptively.

Medical sciences have adopted mind meditation techniques. It reduces stress levels in patients and improves symptoms of various diseases such as depression, anxiety, blood pressure, skin infections, chronic pain, and heart failure.

The complexity of the modern world has paved the way for chronic stress. Meditation has been practiced since ancient times in China and India to relieve stress problems. The writing of Taoism and Confucianism refers to the techniques of stress relief through meditation.

Chinese Roots Of Meditation Hunting

John Kabat Zinn was based on Zen Buddhism in the 19th century the ancient Chinese practiced sophisticated techniques to provide stress, including breathing and meditation. Historians believe that the adherents of Buddhism, Confucianism, and Lao-Tsu have collected their teachings that will serve as a guiding principle for future generations. The peaceful approach allowed the force to cope with the difficulties of war, death, and loss of property.

Taoism appeared during the reign of the Shang dynasty, but the official records of practice and learning did not survive. Lao Tzu began the formal writing of these teachings in Tao Da Ching, the central source of Taoism. Includes 81 separate chapters. Chang-Xie, another text of Tao, was compiled in the 3rd and 4th century

B.C. The Chinese consider the text a social, political, spiritual, and philosophical classic.

Chinese Philosophy And Medicine

In western medicine, the heart is seen as a pump of blood circulation in all parts of the body, while the brain is the thought organ for perception, memory, feelings, intuition, and decision-making. Chinese philosophy does not distinguish the brain and heart. The heart is a spirit that works in tandem with a dynamic environment. The goal is to create harmony between the blue and the environment.

Stress Relief-Confucian Approach

Confucius, a Chinese philosopher, developed this school of thought during the government struggle. He believed that the true happiness of a person depends on social harmony. Its formation is based on the principle that there is a social harmony in which people act responsibly and treat others with respect, empathy, and confidence. He stressed that people should live practically according to an appropriate ethical behavior model. His teachings are designed to ensure a virtuous life with respect and loyalty.

Confucius says that social war and political instability have caused individual stress. He believed that people need to develop social harmony to live a stress-free life. He mentioned the principles that the ruling class should apply to promote social assistance and harmony. Unfortunately, his council did not follow the ruling class.He continues to fight, which imposes problems on ordinary people.

Taoist Philosophy Of Stress Relief

Taoism has proposed triple measures to reduce chronic stress problems.

Jing-Man must be free from prejudices such as norms, values, dichotomies, differences, concepts, judgments, and theories that control his behavior.

Wei has another measure: disrespect for Self-interference with others.

Shi-the third step is to avoid participating in world affairs.

Compliance with these steps requires self-improvement that involves impartial observation and participation in the current environment. Guan refers to a state of receptivity, a calm and clear observation, where he tries to understand himself, the current situation, and business, rather than having an idea of reality. A person experiences Tao in his real state without affecting the attitude of others to the nature of Tao.

When you reach the status of a guano, you create an unbiased view of the world that influences your thoughts, emotions, decisions, and behaviors. You realize that there is no definitive or biased concept and that there are different ways to handle situations. You will realize that you have several options for assessing and managing a particular situation. You realize that you are excluded from the dynamic world by following firm principles that try to escape reality. This moment of consciousness creates harmony with the natural world, therefore an effective source of stress.

The empty blue allows you to experience the Tao for free. Robert Santi, a philosopher, believes that the phenomenon acts as a source of delicate force, allowing a man to act naturally according to the constantly changing needs of nature.

The importance of breathing

The tenth verse for Tae Jing says that we must breathe as a child naturally and uncompromisingly. We need to focus on our breathing and let go of anxious thoughts and emotions. It is necessary to monitor the process of free and simple breathing. Breathing is the main activity of any living being. We breathe for the first time at birth and die with the last breath. Breathing in harmony with nature allows freedom. Limited breathing causes fatigue and tension because Xin experiences a closed, inflexible, harsh, frightening, and hostile nature. This creates stress and paves the way for a brutal breathing cycle.

In the sixth chapter of Chuang Tzu, there was a difference between deep breathing (from the heel) and superficial breathing (from the neck). Shallow breathing is a symptom of confusion, limitation, stress, and negative thoughts, while deep breathing refers to calmness, clarity, and conscious blue. The child experiences free-breathing because he is not affected by tension and other restrictions. In contrast, adults do not have the freedom to breathe.

Space and its advantages

Deep breathing relaxes the body of restrictive thoughts, judgments, and values. It cleans the inner self and balances the energy, allowing them to move freely. Lama Tartang Tulku thinks that this feeling is stronger than the expression of joy; it's huge, deep, and infinite.

Practice Qigong and Buddhist Spirit

The practice of Buddhist consciousness is aimed at disappearance or Anichka. There is a deep connection between the concept of Anik and Qi, a Taoist concept. Mindfulness focuses on mental images, physical feelings, inner speech, and emotional feelings of the body; this makes ordinary experiences unusual. Feelings and thoughts flow like an energy that expands, pulsates, pulls, and vibrates. In turn, Qigong, the practice of internal alchemy involves exercises to create this experience with the flow of energy. The combination of these two practices combines the best of both worlds. Mindfulness routines strengthen attention, the ability to decipher light energy in an ordinary experience. Qigong delicately activates the living energy. Chinese medicine combines hunting as a fluid energy flow through different parts of the body. The disease is caused when pulsatile energy is not enough in the human body.

The practice of Qigong combines these imbalances to eliminate stagnation and create harmony between the flow of energy and the Xin. Ingenuity helps us to openly accept the internal experiences of mind and body, completing the procedures of Qigong. The combination increases potency for deep healing.

Taoism and Stress

In Taoism, we often talk about life that has a "flow" or behaves "like water." "We will achieve this by avoiding and overcoming obstacles and limitations. We do this by relaxing: "we slowly accept things", looking for the flow of the world and going with it. People I've spoken to over the years have asked me what makes laziness different from laziness to stay here and say we all do it. This is a big difference!

Laziness, when a person takes responsibility for what he is responsible for, what needs to be done, or even what he wants to do. This behavior can lead to even more suffering and stress. Laziness literally resists the flow of the world, which is ugly, as if you are doing something wrong all over the world. Relaxation and laziness are two completely different things.

Relax or "float downstream", in the Taoist sense, when we lose our fears, and we are just in the moment. You can be completely relaxed at home, at work, even in a key situation. This is a very important concept. The key doesn't necessarily slow down, because you can't always do it in a key situation. We are trying to do our best and understand that this is what we are doing now and here.

If you take an injured friend to the emergency room, you obviously can't afford to switch off or slow it down. Your duty is to help your friend, and that's why you need to relax in this flow. Fear of driving can lead to a car accident, or worse. It is much more important to stay active and, at this point, be ready to do everything possible to bring your friend to the hospital.

I mean, there's a way to relax in any situation. Exercises that can help you in considering; when you start to feel that stress is attacking your flow when you feel that tension in your shoulder blades, shrinking in temples, think about it.

Why is it so stressful?

It's up to you, but what do you want to do?

Why did he hit you so hard?

Are you sure you're reacting like this?

Can you let it go?

Try to do this the next time you start doing something. Relaxing under pressure, really at the right time, is a skill, which means you can learn and develop it. In fact, you can already have it on one level or another. Find out where your milestone is, where your stress starts to affect you, and starts from there.

To truly understand the Taoist regime, you must first understand a little Taoist belief. Taoism takes place in the heart of East Asia and Chinese cultures and has deep roots in the 2000s, although it only spread to the West in more modern times when people begin to reject materialism for deeper spiritual understanding.

Taoists are humble egos that emphasize compassion, humility, and moderation, while others are emphasized by their minimalist eating habits.

Although Taoism is not known, however, breaks the rules for his opinions inactive care, focuses on the human connection with nature and, therefore, does not believe in the hard way and ordered of modern society, deciding to follow the natural flow of the Universe. The general Taoist terms Yin and Yang refer to the positive and negative energies of the Universe.

Five colors blind eyes.

Five tones muffle the hearing.

Five flavors confuse languages.

Fast horses and exciting hunting make the wild and crazy spirits.

Rare and expensive things make people on the street.

That's why Sage weighs the stomach, not the eye,

he always ignores it and chooses it.

I Gave You Chings, Part 12.

Historically, the Taoist diet consisted mainly of fresh fruits and vegetables, with little meat and no cereals, as they thought, during the process of digestion, creatures like the demon would be freed from the rot of and would try to eat them from the inside. In most modern times, the diet changed and began to be based mainly on the consumption of whole grains and fresh fruits and vegetables according to tradition.

The Taoist diet connects the five main flavors with the elements of nature: sweet (earthy), salty (water), acidic (wood), bitter (fire), spicy (metal). They believe that greed and the rise of one taste on one pedestal on another make you feel the taste, so it is important to balance the flavors to achieve inner harmony.

Taoism is all-natural, and people are part of nature. One of the beliefs most important is "eat food alone" that is, to avoid artificial substances, artificial that the body can not metabolize, and they can contain the flavors unbalanced, like artificial additives, medicines, etc., - highly processed foods that contain little or do not have nutritional value, like white flour, sugar, this is not something that the body should consume and do not grow from the ground, so they are not actually a "food" suitable natural to the human body consumption.

Historically

Most of the classical Taoist literature speaks a lot about the sages of antiquity or people who existed in prehistoric times. Some texts suggest that they exist only when they breathe and do not consume food at all. They lived as born and received food only from the Qi or Yin-Yang of the Universe.

This practice, known as "Bigoo", is sometimes used as part of some Taoist traditions and mythological ideas, but it is not something that is practical or even safe for modern people living in a normal society to try. Taoists believe that man has changed, and since then, the Old State has decreased, which means that it is perfectly acceptable to eat food.

It is believed that the early Taoists had a regime that reflected this vision of wise and enlightened masters even before history and before Agricultural Development. Therefore, in the early traditions, the Taoists did not eat cereals.

There can be several reasons for this, from health problems to compliance with some mythological, agricultural factors of the past, and even other social factors. The minimalist approach is often used to explain this, arguing that the Taoists do not live only from food and unconsciously receive energy from space.

However, as mentioned above, the reason he refuses to eat cereal in many of the first texts is that it does not excite the "three verses."

Three verses

The first mythological explanation of wheat abstinence is three verses.

These are literally three demonic worms that live in the human intestine and are responsible for the disintegration of the body after death.

Of course, since their goal is to devour your body, it is in their interest to die as quickly as possible.

Until death, these three worms will live in the human intestine by eating a rotten biological substance that is digested.

So, when your intestines digested the grain, three worms ate the waste that was produced. When they fed on cereals, they became stronger, and later they could feed on the rest of your body, making you die faster.

Since the longevity of continuing to grow is one of the main goals of many Taoist practices, the purpose of the diet was to "starve"3 verses by reducing the consumption of cereals or completely excluding it.

From a modern point of view, it is possible that the early Taoists just noticed a correlation between caloric intake and aging or poor health.

Assuming that a cell has a finite number of possible divisions during the entire life cycle, it would be necessary to significantly slow the metabolic process to slow down the process of cell division.

Another possibility mentioned earlier is simply a tribute to a docile period when people were not engaged in agriculture and did not participate in social activities and games of excessive food production.

Third immortal, the King says to the King::

"Reach the Tao avoiding all the grains. You will never have to keep up with the rhythm of the Moon and the plant or crop.

In this way, people of mysterious antiquity reached old age because they remained at a minimum and never ate cereals."

As Dai Zhang says (verse of the Great existence):

Of the five seeds, a chisel that shortens life.,

Feel five organs and cut our holes.

One day he got into our stomach,

We no longer have the chance to live long enough.

The goal is to avoid all deaths completely

Keep the intestines without discharge!"

While many ancient Taoists practiced abstinence from cereals, this is not entirely true. There is a lot of evidence that the Taoists ate or literally searched for rice.

Perhaps abstinence from cereals was more a purification process or a kind of fasting that led to important rituals, ceremonies such as taking long-term medications, fasting, taking elixirs, and so on.

Mode

Recently, the typical diet has radically changed to focus primarily on the cereal-based diet rather than practicing complete abstinence from cereals. Even if there are radical people who claim never to eat, they are often ridiculed by the media and then discover that they are "hungry" for attention, not real old-fashioned Taoists.

The modern Taoist diet mainly adheres to the basic theory of Yin-Yang and five elements and relies heavily on unprocessed whole grains, fresh vegetables (especially root vegetables), and very little meat.

It is important that the vegetables are eaten at the exact time of the year and are steamed or fried. The kitchen takes natural goodness. Fruits usually dried or cooked, and the consumption of tropical fruit is incompatible considered unbalanced five fragrances because of its strong, often citrus flavor. It is also important seasonal and without any human intervention.

As a rule, all red and blue meat, including pork, rabbit, snails, and others, should be avoided. Bird and game can be eaten as well as fish. However, fish and other seafood should be consumed only once a week because of the large amount of Yin. Some fish, such as salmon, shark, swordfish, and mackerel, which are very Yin, should be avoided completely.

Drinking alcohol, caffeine, and chewing/smoking tobacco is intended for their refined nature.

The modern Taoist relies on moderation in his eating habits and should try to avoid eating something too much (garlic, ginger, onion, etc.).

Differences Between The Taoist Regime And The Modern Western Regime

In the West, lifestyle and eating habits contributed to a sharp increase in such problems as heart disease, obesity, stress, cancer, arthritis, and so on.

Attention has shifted from initial prevention (a natural, healthy diet) to medication and surgery. However, an ounce of prevention is worth a pound of treatment. Why try to fight the disease, when it is rooted, when, with some simple guidelines, we can avoid it in the first place?

The modern Taoist regime, in contrast to the modern Western regime, is:

Quick overview

High energy

Enriched with vitamins and minerals

Easy digestibility for the body

Raw and processed

This means that daily Western foods such as bread and milk, which we believe are perfectly healthy, and are considered almost poisonous to strict Taoists. Instead, rice and soy milk are used as substitutes, and skim milk is usually taken.

The "Salt Up" Approach

Qigong: refers to a set of Taoist exercises used to maintain and move with Chi (the energy of the Universe). Methods include meditation and focusing on physical movements. This helps maintain physical and mental health.

As a rule, in many types of Taoist Qigong, energy is taken from the Earth. Similarly, the term "carrot" is at the heart of Taijiquan and many Chinese martial arts and Taoism, so historically and in a Taoist context, the country's authorities were considered the best way to get vital energy from food.

Like Taoist Qigong, the Taoist diet emphasizes the "salt" approach to vegetable consumption. This means that the plant should be consumed in a large percentage of the total diet, especially in the underground (root vegetables), compared to a higher one, such as an Apple.

The main reason for this was that ground vegetables have more energy and the ability to supply the body with more Chi. It is believed that potatoes, all kinds of root crops, potatoes, carrots, beets, to name a few, provide good energy to the soil, which helps the spleen (immune system) become stronger, and Jing Qi more "roots."

After all, the plants attached to the ground were as green as cabbage, Chinese cabbage, spinach, and so on, which were often pickled or stored for the winter.

Then came the highest crops: peppers, tomatoes, eggplants, etc., which were used to provide good energy, but on a smaller scale.

Zao Wou-Ki, the deceased Chinese-French painter, joined the art of calligraphy with impressionism by merging eastern and western art. I recently read his obituary, and it made me think about the artistic process and creativity. I wanted to use his life as a starting point for exploring the art and Taoist thinking, in particular, therefore, that his second wife suffered from deep depression and committed suicide.

These different themes intersect in Za's life. As a child, he learned the art of calligraphy is strongly influenced by Taoist philosophy, and when he arrived in Paris in 1948 (before the communist revolution), went with his wife to Paris, where he settled in the same block, in the district of Montparnasse, where Othon communism-a well-known painter in the Fauvist movement was the organization of the dao of movement.

The tragedy of the depression fellon his life when his wife Chu Ching, the star of the Chinese cinema, the great beauty became a critically acclaimed sculptor who committed suicide at the peak of its success. This must have had a significant impact on the emotional content of his paintings

Zao's work was similar in style to the abstract impressionist painters who significantly influenced his thoughts when he visited New York City and said that Matisse, Cezanne, and Picasso were also very influential in their style. Interestingly, when reading his style of painting, there is a big emphasis on western influences, but little on its Chinese roots, in particular the Taoist thinking. In China, calligraphy generally focuses on the proper design of Chinese characters, and the ability to do so was an essential element of Chinese culture, as well as Taoist thinking, so it is impossible to separate the writing from the basic elements of Taoism completely.

One of the main elements of Taoist thinking in relation to Chinese calligraphy and French Impressionists is the role of intuition. This addresses Chuang TSU's great Taoist essay, which told the story of the demonstration of the connection between creativity and intuition, he said, and paraphrased.

Once a carpenter on a bicycle for a trolley in the courtyard of the palace fence. When he looked up, he noticed a strong Duke reading in a nearby room. He laid his instruments, came to the duke, and asked. May I ask What Your Royal Highness reads? The duke replied: "I have read the works of great lords and sages." The Carpenter asked: "Do the wise LIVE?"No," the duke replied, " They died a long time ago."The Carpenter, who asked, even more, asked the duke if they were dead, so the words you read are just sequins left by the Ancients. The duke became increasingly angry, looked firmly at the Carpenter, and replied: "I read and got angry." What does the bicycle manufacturer know about books or knowledge? Your questions are offensive. You better explain it to me. If you can defend your point of view, I'll let you go, and if you can't, I'll have you killed.'

"Without fear," Carpenter replied. Let me tell you something about Carpenter's work. If I make the Rays too tight, they don't fit the wheel, and if I release them, the wheel falls off. I have to adapt to perfection. I have power in my hands, and I judge my intuition. In the process, there is an element that can not be described in words. I can not teach my child this intuitive element, nor teach him himself. Here I am at the age of seventy years, living master of the art manufacturing bicycles. The old masters died a long time ago, and that something could not describe the communication that died with them. That's Why Your Majesty reads the drunkenness of an old man.'

Now Zao has died, and as the former master of his art, he can be considered a bullet that escapes the ancients. He took his genius with him, but we can experience the Masterpiece grass on the canvas.

Lewis Harrison is a pioneering author, speaker, and practical philosopher specializing in human potential and personal development.

Lewis runs Life coaching and two residential shelters at the Harrison Center for personal development in Stamford, NY.

Chinese Philosophies Amidst Political Turmoil

In response to the political turmoil associated with the Warring States period in China (403-221 p.No, email.), there were different schools of thought. Among them are Confucianism, Taoism, and the arrival of the silk road, and Buddhism. One can understand and resist the two root philosophies and recognize the reasons why Confucianism was finally approved by the government and not by Taoism. However, both may not be practiced exclusively. Understanding this, one can understand why Mahayana Buddhism, in the form of Chan, began to compete with Confucianism around the 19th century.

Confucianism was conceived and named after Kong Fuza (551-479 BC), known as the philosopher Kong, to his disciples and Confucius in the West. Like his contemporary, the Buddha Siddharta Guatama did not deal with metaphysical problems. His rationale was that guesses about these issues have nothing to do with the ethical, moral, or political scene, but are therefore useless. He believed that the right balance of these three important topics would seem easy by improving individual human relations, and would even reject public Affairs as symptoms of this basic disease: inadequate human relations. Educating people and turning them into Jun or higher persons would help progress in the development of human relations. These people would be official in an ideal government. As the Chinese adopted the philosophy of merging the Congo as a substitute for legalism, the government even encouraged its education system in an attempt to produce junze.

Taoism emphasizes the reconciliation of our human consciousness with the nature of everything or the Tao. Taoism was attributed to a person known as Lao Tzu. Although the purportedly written text, the Tao-da Ching (classics on the road and virtue) was also known as Lao Tzu, so it is currently impossible to determine whether Lao Tzu exists. Most likely, there were four different hands Century he had despite the fact that Lao Tzu, the modern Kong Fuzi, is said to live in the 19th century. Lao Tzu, whose name can be translated as "old teacher" was considered archived in one of the small kingdoms. In Taoist practice, this can be realized by the idea of Wei Wu-Wei, or by an action without actions that can be understood as if it were done without understanding. Once this is done, one agrees with the Tao. This idea is very similar to Congo Fuzi's idea that the characters will automatically restore their human relationships and come into harmony with the basic virtue of Rene's humanity. When asked to explain this idea, Kong Fuzi refused because, like Tao, the Ren that can be described is not the real REN. Unclear. The emphasis on Taoism is more mystical, while Confucianism focuses on ethical and political applications. Neither of them excludes the other, and they are both known to practice government officials in the evening after performing their duties in the workplace.

These two philosophies served to harmonize individuals and society in a certain way. Taoism is really an individual experience, and by definition, it cannot be shared with others. If all people understood the Tao, people would become autonomous, and the problems of the day would collapse as stupidity. This idea is utopian, it is theoretically beautiful, but not practical, and for this, that Confucianism was adopted by the Chinese government, as it deals with issues of more land-based ethics and politics, but with the same basic ideas that are labeled differently. This seemed more relevant to the average person and their problems. In the end, he found an opponent in Buddhism.

Buddhism has an idea similar to Jun, called a Buddha or Bodhisattva. The equivalent of a Confucian troglodyte will be cultivated based on the practice of the noble eight. This path leads to wisdom and compassion, which are synonymous with virtue. This aspect of Buddhism is very similar to Confucianism, and the prospect of the end of suffering in the Four Noble Truths would be very attractive to professionals of this kind of philosophy who did not pay attention to such thoughts. Due to the lack of emphasis on political Affairs and subsequent entry into China was Buddhism, the government never sanctioned as much as Confucianism.

These three forms in question arose or were adopted due to the political chaos of the warring states in the 18th and 4th centuries. In China. Each philosophy is very similar but has its own special differences that are subject to different applications in the enterprise. All survive to this day.

There are two points of view that determine the quality of leadership. Internal factors include character traits and resulting behaviors; external factors include leadership and follower context. Researchers of Behavioral Research believe that internal factors of character, personality, and behavior affect external factors. However, another school believes that external factors affect the leadership process. Modern scientists emphasize the importance of internal factors of leaders and followers: their knowledge, cognition, and experience affect leadership.

New theories about leadership try to suggest that factors of intrinsic character with their resulting behavior significantly affect the essence of leadership. Relative leadership theories emphasize the importance of external and internal factors for effective leadership. Interaction between leaders and their supporters plays an important role in determining the quality of leadership. Skeptics criticize all theories about leadership on the basis of insufficient evidence and questionable leadership techniques.

Taoism generates awareness of the Universe, of humanity and its connection with nature. The philosophy emphasizes that any universal phenomenon consists of interdependent factors, but at the same time competing in nature. Taoists believe that leadership is a process that exists in human society and is based on human relations with the masses. So, you cannot ignore the basics of Taoism, which need a balanced, constantly changing, and interdependent relationship between two contradicting inner forces.

A careful analysis of different theories about leadership suggests that leadership styles are based on the principles of Taoism. The Taoist leadership position believes that leaders and followers share interchangeable relationships, not because leaders follow their leaders and obey as followers; the situation could change over time. External factors are competitive in a single system of leadership or dictatorship. In small leadership systems, internal and external forces work together.

Scientists distinguish two Yang-Yin systems: context and leadership contribute to the relationship between environmental factors and organizational factors. Another system, which includes followers and leaders, develops a smaller Yang-Yin system. Taoism considers the context, and the guidelines should be the same as some parts of the leadership system as related issues that have a broader context are related to a broader leadership style. Regardless of the severity of the context, there are final problems that affect a certain leadership.

Taoism sees human society as a smaller system than the Yang-Yin universe. Each person represents the Yang and Yin microsystem. Taoism States: "humanity follows the rules of the Earth, which in turn follow the rules of heaven (or the Universe). The sky (or the Universe) follows the rules of the Tao, and the Tao follows its nature " (Xiong, 2005)."

The process of Yang and Yin does not repeat itself but occurs in an ascending or descending cycle. Leaders and followers can take Yang and Yin positions at different stages of the development cycle. Every object in the Universe undergoes eternal change. Leadership research begins the study of individual traits and goes back to new theories based on transformative, visionary, and charismatic changes in personality.

Taoism considers dynamic leadership by nature. This allows leaders and followers to exercise dominance of power. The balance in the strength of the two entities is short-lived. Yang is a dynamic and active force, while Yin is a calm and passive force. Leaders are seen as Yang when they show power proactively and progressively, while disciples act as Yin when they are less active and passive. Otherwise, leaders are Yin when they do not actively participate, and followers are Yang when they actively participate in growth and success. The dominant strength of the organization determines leadership. The nature of leadership determines which power currently dominates the organization. So, we will consider this point in more detail when we look at successful models of leader traits based on Taoism.

Success Stories of Taoist Leadership

To understand dynamic leadership, a model of the fundamental traits of a successful leader based on Taoist principles was created. The model reflects dynamic leadership, as well as the leadership theories that have managed to follow this model. This model assumes that there are five main traits for developing a successful leader.

Successful leaders at the child stage of the organization must have the characteristics of Yan, that is, initiatives and progressive. At this stage, the leader must win the support and faith of his supporters, who, in turn, must understand the mission and vision of the organization. The child's installation requires the participation of all its members; the leader must show care, love, and, most importantly, listen to his followers. It solves the small mistakes of its followers by encouraging them to be creative and increase innovation. Since it requires everyone to contribute, it is not strict and collects advice from followers. He consciously supports good talents, taking care of their desires and needs to achieve personal success. Leadership achieves rapid growth for its organization by leveraging the innovative and creative abilities of its followers. He is praised for his charisma and recognition of his success.

The second stage of the organization's growth is associated with rapid development, which the leader sees in a fiery position. The organization is entering a strong phase of the Jan. Managers are energetic and enthusiastic about the success of the organization and are active at every step. They are implementing new strategies to increase the bandwidth of their subscribers to increase the growth and revenue of a successful organization. Any successful business venture is the result of the continuing progressive efforts of its leader.

Taoism, however, believes that the leader should display the qualities of accuracy in the second stage. The leader is in a strong position in relation to his supporters. The rapid success of an organization can overwhelm leaders, thereby encouraging them to practice some unrealistic programs that followers can't object to. At the moment, many companies have failed because of unrealistic goals. Thus, the leader must achieve realistic goals with precision, enthusiasm, and encouragement.

The third stage sees the leaders in the position of the Earth, the stage of maturity institution. Leaders have a stable growth perspective, and a balance between supporters and leadership is being established. Harmony reaches its ideal state by enjoying stable and effective communication relationships. Taoism believes that the leader at this stage demonstrates loyalty. A leader is an honest person who is true to his responsibility and maintains transparency with his followers. He adopts a democratic leadership style in which followers can easily predict his behavioral line. Understanding the leader and his supporters are the most important factor in the success of an organization.

However, at this stage, different approaches can be applied to achieve success. Despite the balance, the leader can choose to convince the follower to accept his views. Also, the leader can become more democratic, give value to followers, and exchange opinions, motivating their contributions. Some leaders may allow followers to provide their best efforts. This allows you to listen to the advice provided by followers. At the moment, the leader acts as an intermediary in relation to the driving force of the organization.

The fourth stage of the organization's development puts the leader in the position of metal. The company is experiencing its maturity and is beginning to decline. The organization is governed by a rigid structure, and organizational functions are not active. The leader adopts a conservative leadership style that scares creative followers. Some smart followers are enjoying this situation and exploring their own business. To succeed at this stage, a leader needs characteristics of managerial skills, fairness, regulation, and adequate power to motivate followers and improve their contribution. It requires responsibility, the capability of rewarding followers, and berating the selfish followers.

The last stage of leadership is the water stage, in which the organization reaches the dying stage. The organization loses the support of its creative followers, and the company reaches the transition between birth and death. A wise leader, currently working well. This creates an encouraging prospect of solving current problems, convincing its followers to solve problems, and promise a bright future. Create a new vision for creating a new organization to win the trust of the faithful. It presents visionary skills to encourage capable followers.

However, Taoist principles only act as a basis for classifying fundamental theories of leadership. Since there are many factors that are currently being developed in a leadership model, we need countless theories to understand the characteristics of a true leader. Taoism claims that leadership styles are dynamic due to constantly changing external and internal factors. A theory can explain events that fit a particular pattern; however, the cycle undergoes continuous changes, so several theories take time. There is no definitive theory that can accurately classify different leadership styles.

Researchers now isolate the factors of leadership to the changing contexts, drawing conclusions from an isolated point of view. Because they do not take into account external and internal contexts, leadership theories are not relevant to real events. Despite their limitations, modern leadership theories should not be dismissed as garbage. Modern theories are an integration of the principles of all leadership theories.

This requires that leaders demonstrate appropriate traits in accordance with changing situations. Leadership develops in Yang in some cases of leadership and Yin in other stages. Hey, he should change his behavior accordingly. For example, in water and on land, the leader must show the behavior of an observer. It should accept changes in the organizational structure and not follow the same behavior that is practiced in the early stages. The Taoist principle effectively describes real events, so the boss comes to a reasonable decision.

The Tao te Ching verse offers an effective working principle for successful leaders. He says: "If you want to be a great leader, you need to learn to follow the Tao.

A leader who follows Taoist principles should abandon strict strategies and concepts and define them. Instead of following a complex concept, the leader follows his natural instincts, and his actions are governed by the principles of nature. This time, it may be absurd for a person who retreats into strategic leadership. Taoist principles believe that planning is not as effective as it allows businesses to operate independently. This will be a term for understanding this rare type of leadership since this method is no better than strategic planning.

Do not limit

The Taoist leader allows his supporters to function without any restrictions. The ban of any kind removes the virtues and creativity of followers. This can lead to aggressive outbursts of followers, and a sense of insecurity enters the mind of followers.

Confidence

Taoism believes that the leader must be autonomous. Followers must feel safe, which means that they need everything they need to maintain their existence. Followers must be motivated to take responsibility for their activities and not to be constantly monitored. This is in conflict with a radical approach that leaders are trying to control their subordinates, place to force them to grow on their own. Followers must have the skills to be less dependent on their superiors.

Prohibition Of Law

Tao Te Jing says that in the absence of strict rules, laws, and regulations, supporters adopt an honest work ethic. He believes abandoning Economic Planning will make people richer. Freedom of will and control is better than leadership, which exercises control through policies, plans, retaliatory measures, and rules. But a Leader who does not voluntarily exercise control guarantees better control in an organization that believes in self-government. This allows the principles of Tao to rule the people. The leader must trust the abilities of DAO. Order can be maintained even without strategic and political plans. The leader must give up spending on strategic planning and policy development.

An important question was whether these tools are constructive or harmful to the organization. Modern business leaders develop short-term policies and strategic plans due to market dynamics and geopolitics. The overall benefit can naturally come from the ever-changing dynamics that leaders need to consider.

Taoism believes that the leader simply does not interfere in the affairs of the world and encourages others to follow his example. The goal of obtaining a common advantage allows the leader to apply the principles of Taoism in his Organization.

Wei Wu Wei

Taoism explains the general principles for solving the concept of modern leadership. Taoist philosophers determined the basic characteristics of the leader and explained the strategic directions for many human activities. Activities range from the management of state affairs, with the culture of virtues and morals of people. Thus, understanding the Taoist principles of leadership is excellent information. The Taoists believe that the leaders are no different from the disciples. A person who most serves his people is considered a leader. The principle of Wei wu Wei emphasized spontaneous leadership in a natural way. Respects the natural course of events without any interference. The holistic view of the Tao allows individuals to consider themselves as part of the Universe, thereby cooperating with the natural rhythm of life.

Wei Wu Wei consists of three principles of leadership management. The first principle is to "do something without doing something else."The second principle allows the natural flow of events with non-interference. The third principle concerns symbolic leadership. 10097 words

Chapter 60 Tao Te Ching states: "the leadership of a large organization or state is like cooking small fish."As well as excessive mixing adversely affects the preparation of small fish, excessive interference of imbalance in the workplace. To cultivate the principles of the Tao, the leader must allow natural events to create challenges and naturally explore solutions. The natural flow allows the Tao to harmonize with all things or individuals. The practice of positive inactivity, that is, Wei Wu Wei, allows events to monitor its natural course to respect universal forces. Leaders must adhere to the basic principles and adapt to the constantly changing dynamics of nature. Leaders must agree between non-interference the natural flow of events and efforts to change the natural flow.

There are four types of leadership qualities. The leader strategically manages his supporters and allows them to work independently without interrupting their activities. In addition, the leader is human; that is, cares about the needs of his disciples. Another type of leader carries out punishment and control through policies, rules, and regulations. The fourth type of leader does not believe in Taoist principles, and his supporters despise him. The best form of leadership is the first type, which is based on the Wei Wu Wei ideology of Taoism.

Western Management Theory Vs. Taoism

Douglas McGregor has developed leading theories, namely Theory X and Theory Y. Theory X believes in a leadership style that applies compliance and control. Leaders take different situations, such as followers avoid work, how they do not like, they do not feel that they need to be guided; they are ready to accept responsibility, and therefore demand supervision to achieve organizational goals. The theory promotes a leadership style focused on people management through engagement, delegation, and cooperation. This theory believes that followers are eager to take their responsibilities; they are ready to work and take initiatives to achieve the goals of the organization. Followers help their leaders achieve their goals through positive reinforcement.

McGregor developed another theory, known as Theory Y. This highlights management or leadership through contribution, cooperation, and delegation. According to Theory Y, people want to work; they are willing to accept responsibility, and are ambitious and show initiative to achieve the goal. People can achieve goals with positive motivation.

Abraham Maslow promoted the theory of hierarchical needs. It is largely influenced by Taoist principles and emphasizes self-realization and human dignity. Maslow believes that any style of individual leadership affects only a few cases. The Taoist Leader is far from having the power to teach his disciples. A direct link between Taoism and human psychology can be found through the concept of leadership developed by Maslow.

But there are some consequences of the Taoist leadership.

First, modern researchers are less aware of Maslow's theory of leadership. Taoism offers a broad perspective for academic, social, and behavioral purposes. Secondly, Taoism helps modern leaders practice effective leadership. Taoism can fill the void in the Western philosophy of people management. Third, research studies based on Taoist leadership emphasize the empirical examination of social, behavioral, and Management Sciences. In addition, studies on Taoism reduce human conflicts. Taoist principles create the harmony of themselves with nature and other living beings. Today's world resembles a global village, and residents are engaged in many human and ecological interests. Perhaps Taoism is the most valuable asset for the world's population.

Taoist Tai Chi For a Change, Getting Real Peace

Taoist tai chi is a soft martial art (in China, it is called internal art) that guarantees the well-being and health of people of all colors.

Millions of people, both Asian and others, enjoy the health benefits of the Taoist practice of Tai Chi. It is estimated that there are more than 500 specialized schools for the preparation of sand for this particular style, located in twenty-five countries around the world. Although it has existed for hundreds of years in China and Japan, the Taoist Tai Chi in the 1970s was brought to North America by master Mo Lin-Shin.

The main goal of the Taoist is to strengthen and restore health. It is one of the mildest forms of Taiji and is ideal for the elderly and for those who regain strength for exercise. The movements are slow, thoughtful, and graceful, and their design should help the student develop strength and flexibility.

The practice of Taoist also helps with joint and muscle pain, as it emphasizes twists and subtle strokes. It is also useful for increasing muscle strength and improving blood circulation in the body. It also helps people who tremble or dizzy to restore a sense of balance.

The exercises are also intended to help you relieve stress and anxiety through delicate activities. It is sometimes called "Meditation in motion" because the continuity of movement combined with a sense of attention helps to heal and rejuvenate the mind and body. Since this practice is based on meditation and learning simultaneously, Taoist tai chi is also known as a regenerating form of delicate exercises.

The physical component of the Taoist Taiji consists of basic principles known as "fundamentals". The whole set of bases consists of one hundred and eight movements. Some of these movements mimic the positions of the army or animals found in nature, which is typical of all species of Taiji. However, these movements are not necessarily as aggressive as very old frame styles like Chen Tai Chi style.

The general spiritual intention of the Taoist is to develop an inner sense of peace, wisdom, and knowledge that puts a person in a spiritually powerful position to spread compassion and generosity to others. The goal of this is to lose all ego and egocentrism through the practice of this ancient art of "meditation in motion."

Taoist tai chi can be somewhat compared to Alexander's technique, which focuses on relaxation, breathing, balance, posture, spine alignment, angle correction, weight transfer tracking, spiral rotations, limb detection and closure, tail bone centering, and spine stretching and alignment. Movements are soft and circular; they are performed with a concentrated but relaxed state of mind.

A key aspect of the Taoist is the acceptance of the spirit of dedication, kindness, and elimination of selfishness. Taoist tai chi is not only practiced but lives, your life can change. Perhaps constant changes will not happen overnight, and it is better to know them by their example, showing life in harmony, compassion, and service to others.

Taoist Meditations For Healing

Taoists in China have, for thousands of years, used acupuncture, herbs, exercise, and meditation to promote health and prolong life. The techniques they have honed over the centuries are, perhaps surprisingly, perfectly suited to our modern health problems.

Taoist meditation is also easy to do for many modern people, because it engages the mind more than other meditation styles, such as watching the breath.

Taoists mainly use meditation as a spiritual practice to become one with the Tao. However, noting the health benefits of meditation, they developed techniques specifically to improve health. Health and longevity have always been important to the Taoists for two reasons. First, they needed time and energy to focus on their spiritual practices. The second reason is that some sects believed in physical immortality, so they were looking for ways to extend their lives indefinitely.

Most Taoist healing meditations make use of the energy theory of acupuncture. Skilled meditators can manipulate I.Q., or vital energy, as effectively as an acupuncturist can. In addition to the flow of qi in the meridians, the Taoists have a chakra system, very similar to the Indian one, as well as a five-element system.

The five elements are energy categories. All nature is divided into one of the five elements. Each organ and tissue in your body is also divided into five elements. For example, the wooden element is associated with the liver, gallbladder, tendons and ligaments, and eyes. Psychologically, it is associated with planning and organization, flexibility, anger, and frustration. It is the system most vulnerable to stress. Externally, it is related to the spring season, wind, and green color.

Taoist meditation can include movement, sound, and/or display of colored light to clean and heal each of the five elements. If you have a problem-related wood element, you can breathe fresh green light into the area, and imagine toxic energy coming out like smoke with your breath out. Where ever the problem is, it is useful to start breathing the green light into the liver until it is glowing green.

In Taoism, there are three main chakras or energy centers in the body. One just below the navel, one in the center of the chest and one between the eyes. A simple visualization of healing is to become aware of the problem in your body. Give it a shape and color. So, imagine moving it to the nearest Energy Center, and then out of your body. Let it soar a few inches from your from the Energy Center. Then, as you exhale, imagine the white light blowing through that object. With each breath, the object fades until it disappears completely.

Taoist meditation, as Bruce Kumar Francis teaches, offers a way to give everyone lasting peace and a strong sense of belonging to the world. But the type of meditation system is very different from the one that most people are used to.

We use what Bruce calls the Taoist method of water. Many meditation techniques can be classified as "fire Techniques.""This means that these systems tend to cause or "burn" the negative mental and emotional effects of everyday life on this material.

On the other hand, the "water method" allows these effects to wear out gently like "water ice and carbonated water."Just as the flow gradually and gently separates the heaviest substances, this method can eliminate all the collected shit in your body and mind.

This amazing system begins with a set of moving Qigong called dragon & Tiger Qigong and the silence inherent in the "long-term breathing" method. Both deep systems are designed to start more advanced practices in the Taoist water method.

In addition, the practice of the short form of the Wu Tai Chi-Chuan family system (Taijiquan) and the single and double Palm will change with the Taoist art of change, Ba Gua Chang (Baguazhan) will be studied to bring the student to a higher level of integration with the Universe.

So, I cannot answer the question of whether Taoist meditation can bring you peace. Everything is in you. I can tell you that the Taoist method of water will give you the tools to get there.

Taoism has developed various exercises to develop and improve its sexual strength. A technique passed down from generation to generation is called "deer exercise."In fact, it is a simple exercise for rubbing and anal contraction with such advantages as:

1. Strengthens the tissues of the genitals

2. It improves blood circulation and transports nutrients from sperm to the rest of the body

3. Replenishes energy in any weakened gland

4. Build sexual stamina

So how do you do this exercise? You will need to perform this exercise in the morning after waking up and in the evening, just before bedtime. This can be done standing, sitting, or even lying down.

To perform the deer exercise, vigorously rub your hands to get warmth and energy from your body. Now quickly take your right hand and gently close your testicles(it works best when you are not wearing anything). Now place your left hand on your belly (which is two inches below your navel) and rub it at a relaxed and pleasant pace counterclockwise 81 times.

When you are done, vigorously rub your hands again and start again; the difference this time is that you change the position of the hands (the left hand destroys the testicles and the right abdomen Clockwise).

The Taoists are very focused on the use of mental concentration in their exercises. So it is not surprising that mental concentration is also part of the exercise. According to the Taoists, focusing your mind at some point on, you will effectively bring I.Q.to this point.

Therefore, when rubbing, you need to pay all your attention to physical movements and increasing heat. Then, when your hand touches the testicles and abdomen, feel the Qi move from the hand to the testicles and abdomen.

Deer exercise is designed to be effective if you practice it every day morning and evening. However, if you want to see instant results, you can try taking herbal supplements. Herbal supplements are the safest and most effective way to last more than 20 minutes and have an effect that lasts for several days. This makes it the most popular and economical method of staying firm and lasting for a long time.

The Extraordinary Taoist Water Method

The Taoist water method, as I learned from Bruce Kumar Francis, gives every person who practices it with great honesty and humility the opportunity to integrate body, mind, and spirit into the body of the entire cosmos.

This system usually begins with an honest student learning a gentle but deep method of breathing known to some as "longevity breathing."As the name suggests, it is designed to extend the number of its years, providing a quality of life that is little present in those who are old.

From here, the next step is an often surprising set of medical Qigong, commonly referred to as "Dragon and Tiger qigong."This short group of exercises without influence is often taught to cancer patients in China.

In my school, I teach the famous eight brocades of Qigong (Babajan), which reportedly dates back to the Ming dynasty. I learned about this famous set from my teacher Shifu Lo Dexu, a man of incredible strength and skill.

Next in the Taoist water method is the "opening of the energy doors of the body" set neigong. Neigong stands for internal learning and is crucial for learning the incredible transformational arts of Tai Chi, Bagua, and sin II.

This system continues with the advanced ensembles Union of Heaven and Earth, Body Arch Bend, and immortal high levels playing in the clouds. It is beyond the scope of this short article to describe these sets well enough to give them justice. I hope you have enjoyed this brief introduction to the Taoist water method as much as I have written.

Printed in Dunstable, United Kingdom

64808317R00078